Heinrich Bullinger
and the Doctrine
of Predestination

Texts and Studies in Reformation and Post-Reformation Thought

General Editor
Prof. Richard A. Muller, Calvin Theological Seminary

Caspar Olevianus, *A Firm Foundation: An Aid to Interpreting the Heidelberg Catechism,* translated, with an introduction by Lyle D. Bierma.

John Calvin, *The Bondage and Liberation of the Will: A Defence of the Orthodox Doctrine of Human Choice against Pighius,* edited by A. N. S. Lane, translated by G. I. Davies.

Law and Gospel: Philip Melanchthon's Debate with John Agricola of Eisleben over Poenitentia, by Timothy J. Wengert.

Martin Luther as Prophet, Teacher, and Hero: Images of the Reformer, 1520–1620, by Robert Kolb.

Melanchthon in Europe: His Work and Influence beyond Wittenberg, edited by Karin Maag.

Reformation and Scholasticism: An Ecumenical Enterprise, edited by Willem J. van Asselt and Eef Dekker.

The Binding of God: Calvin's Role in the Development of Covenant Theology, by Peter A. Lillback.

Divine Discourse: The Theological Methodology of John Owen, by Sebastian Rehnman.

Heinrich Bullinger and the Doctrine of Predestination: Author of "the Other Reformed Tradition"? by Cornelis P. Venema.

Heinrich Bullinger and the Doctrine of Predestination

Author of "the Other Reformed Tradition"?

Cornelis P. Venema

4863

Baker Academic

A Division of Baker Book House Co
Grand Rapids, Michigan 49516

Published by Baker Academic
a division of Baker Book House Company
P.O. Box 6287, Grand Rapids, MI 49516-6287

Printed in the United States of America

Library of Congress Cataloging-in-Publication Data

Venema, Cornelis P.
    Heinrich Bullinger and the doctrine of predestination : author of "the other reformed tradition"? / Cornelis P. Venema
        p.   cm. — (Texts and studies in Reformation and post-Reformation thought)
    Includes bibliographical references and index.
    ISBN 0-8010-2605-9 (pbk.)
    1. Bullinger, Heinrich, 1504–1575—Contributions in doctrine of predestination. 2. Predestination—History of doctrines—16th century. I. Title. II. Series.
    BT809 .V46 2002
    234′.9′092—dc21   2002016483

For information about Baker Academic, visit our web site:
www.bakeracademic.com

To Joseph, Charissa, Rachel and Carolyn
Each one a blessing from the Lord
(Psalm 128)

Contents

Series Preface 9
Preface...11
List of Abbreviations 15

1. Bullinger—Author of "the Other Reformed Tradition"?...........17
   A. The Older Literature: Comparing Bullinger and Calvin on
      Predestination...20
   B. The Debate Regarding Calvin's Doctrine of
      Predestination...23
   C. More Recent Literature: Bullinger as Covenant
      Theologian 27
   D. Procedure and Outline of This Study 32

2. Bullinger's Doctrine of Predestination, 1536-1556................35
   A. Bullinger's *Oratio* of 1536..36
   B. The *Decades* of 1549-1551 41
   C. The *Summa Christlicher Religion* of 1556.........................49
   D. Summary..53

3. Bullinger's Correspondence on Predestination, 1551-1553....57
   A. Correspondence with Calvin Concerning Bolsec...............58
   B. Correspondence with Bartholomäus Traheronus, 1553.....63
   C. Summary...68

4. Bullinger's Participation in Two Conflicts over
   Predestination, 1560-1561...71
   A. Peter Martyr Vermigli and the Doctrine of Predestination..72
   B. The Conflict Between Vermigli and Bibliander, 1560.........75
   C. The Zürich *Gutachten* on Predestination of 1561...............79
   D. Summary...86

5. Bullinger's Doctrine of Predestination in the Second Helvetic
   Confession...89
   A. The Place of Predestination Within the Confession...........91
   B. The Doctrine of Predestination in the Confession.............95
   C. Summary...97

6. Assessing Whether Bullinger Authored "the Other Reformed Tradition"... 101
   A. Bullinger's Doctrine of Predestination: Homiletical Augustinianism.. 101
   B. Bullinger on Predestination and Covenant: Another Reformed Tradition?... 107
   C. Summary 118

Bibliography 121
Index 131

Series Preface

The heritage of the Reformation is of profound importance to the church in the present day. Yet there remain many significant gaps in our knowledge of the intellectual development of Protestantism in the sixteenth century, and there are not a few myths about the theology of the Protestant orthodox writers of the late sixteenth and seventeenth centuries. These gaps and myths, frequently caused by ignorance of the scope of a particular thinker's work, by negative theological judgments passed on the theology of the Reformers or their successors by later generations, or by an intellectual imperialism of the present that singles out some thinkers and ignores others regardless of their relative significance to their own times, stand in the way of a substantive encounter with this important period in our history. Understanding and appropriation of that heritage can occur only through the publication of significant works—monographs and sound, scholarly translations—that present the breadth and detail of the thought of the Reformers and their successors.

Texts and Studies in Reformation and Post-Reformation Thought proposes to make available such works as Caspar Olevianus's *Firm Foundation,* Theodore Beza's *Table of Predestination,* and Jerome Zanchi's *Confession of Faith,* together with significant monographs on traditional Reformed theology, under the guidance of an editorial board of recognized scholars in the field. Major older works, like Heppe's *Reformed Dogmatics,* will be reprinted or reissued with new introductions. These works, moreover, are intended to address two groups: an academic and a confessional or churchly audience. The series recognizes the need for careful, scholarly treatment of the Reformation and of the era of Protestant orthodoxy, given the continuing presence of misunderstandings particularly of the later era in both the scholarly and the popular literature as well as the recent interest in reappraising the relationship of the Reformation to Protestant orthodoxy. In addition, however, the series hopes to provide the church at large with worthy documents from its rich heritage and thereby to support and to stimulate interest in the roots of the Protestant tradition.

Richard A. Muller

9

Preface

The original stimulus for this monograph began with a Reformation research seminar on Heinrich Bullinger at Princeton Theological Seminary. The seminar was led by Professor Edward A. Dowey, Jr., who instilled in me a lasting interest in the reforming labor and contributions of Bullinger as Zwingli's successor in Zürich. Prior to taking this course, I was largely unaware of the contributions of Bullinger to the development and formation of the Reformed tradition in the sixteenth century and beyond. If history belongs to those who tell its story, then those who have told the story of the Reformation of the sixteenth century have often given short shrift to figures like Bullinger and other "Reformers in the Wings."[1] My study of Bullinger's contribution to the Reformation of the sixteenth century has only confirmed my initial impression that his life and thought demand greater attention than they have received in the past.

The focus of this monograph is the doctrine of predestination in Bullinger's theology, particularly the question whether his doctrine substantially differed from the Reformed tradition as represented by its leading figure, John Calvin of Geneva. Students of the history of doctrine are well aware of the importance of the subject of predestination and election to Reformation theology. In the service of the theme of *sola gratia,* the Reformers of the sixteenth century embraced the Augustinian theological and exegetical tradition with its emphasis upon the divine initiative in the accomplishment of salvation. Human salvation begins, not with the creature's turning toward the Triune God in faith and repentance, but with the Creator's gracious and merciful turning toward the creature. Salvation, from its conception in the divine counsel to its administration through the preaching of the gospel, is God's gracious gift, not a human achievement. Bullinger, as much as Calvin and many others, was an articulate exponent of this Augustinian theological heritage.

However, in the literature on the history of doctrine in the emerging Reformed tradition of the sixteenth and seventeenth centuries, the claim has taken hold that the Reformed doctrines of predestination and covenant represent two quite divergent ways of

1. I borrow this language from the fine collection of essays of David C. Steinmetz, *Reformers in the Wings* (1971; reprint, Grand Rapids: Baker, 1981).

articulating the theme of *sola gratia*. J. Wayne Baker and others have argued that, contrary to the emphasis upon sovereign and unconditional predestination in the Reformed tradition stemming from John Calvin, the Rhineland Reformers, beginning with Zwingli and including Bullinger, authored another Reformed tradition. This tradition's primary emphasis was upon a conditional covenant doctrine. Bullinger, it is argued, was the author of a Reformed tradition that repudiated the double predestinarianism of Calvin and advocated instead a single or conditional predestinarianism. Whereas Calvin and Geneva followed the tradition of predestinarian doctrine stemming from Augustine, Bullinger and Zürich were responsible for a quite different formulation of the doctrine of grace, one which by means of its covenant view lends more weight to the realization of God's purposes in history. These distinct doctrinal positions of Calvin and Bullinger constitute the historical background to a divergence within subsequent Reformed theology between unconditional predestinarianism and conditional covenantalism. The tradition of covenant theology, authored in significant measure by Bullinger, actually represents a substantial departure from historic Augustinianism on the doctrine of grace.

The purpose of the following monograph is to evaluate this claim and to provide a careful analysis of Bullinger's doctrine of predestination. In order to accomplish this purpose, the study begins with an introductory chapter, outlining the history of the interpretation and debate respecting Bullinger's doctrine of predestination in relation to the doctrine of his contemporaries. The following chapters, which constitute the heart of the study, trace in historical order the most significant writings of Bullinger on the subject of predestination. Chapter 2 treats three systematic statements of the doctrine, written during the early and middle stages of Bullinger's life. Chapter 3 considers two significant pieces of correspondence, which directly address Bullinger's appraisal of Calvin's doctrine. Chapter 4 analyzes Bullinger's involvements in two controversies in Zürich toward the end of Bullinger's service as *Antistes* or chief pastor in Zürich. Chapter 5 reviews a comprehensive statement of Bullinger's theology, the Second Helvetic Confession, which represents Bullinger's mature expression of the Reformed and catholic faith. After having traced Bullinger's writings on the doctrine of predestination throughout his life, the final chapter draws some conclusions regarding Bullinger's doctrine, its distinction from that of Calvin, and the thesis that he authored another Reformed tradition.

There are several acknowledgements that I should like to make in connection with the publication of this monograph. In addition to the original encouragement given to me by professor Dowey, I am grateful to Richard Muller for his interest in this study and for his willingness to consider it for publication in the series, Texts and Studies in Reformation and Post-Reformation Thought. I also wish to thank the editors of *The Sixteenth Century Journal* who granted me permission to incorporate an earlier article in slightly revised form as chapter 4 of this monograph ("Heinrich Bullinger's Correspondence on Calvin's Doctrine of Predestination," *SCJ* 17/4 [1986]: 435-50). During the course of my research for this study, I was able to make use of the resources available from the Joseph Regenstein Library of the University of Chicago and the H. Henry Meeter Center for Calvin Studies. I thank the staff of these institutions, including Karin Maag, Director of the Meeter Center, for their ready assistance in obtaining certain sources at my request. I am indebted as well to Jacques Roets, pastor of the Cornerstone United Reformed Church of Sanborn, Iowa, and to my daughter, Charissa Venema, for their assistance in preparing the author and subject index. I am also grateful for the assistance of Amy Nemecek, Sarah Smith, Florence Kooiman, Kyle Sorensen and colleague J. Mark Beach in the editing and preparation of my manuscript for publication.

Abbreviations

Confessio Heinrich Bullinger. *Confessio et exposito simplex orthodoxae fide.* In *Bekenntnisschriften und Kirchenordnungen der nach Gottes Wort reformierten Kirche.* Ed. Wilhelm Niesel. Zürich: Zollikon, 1938. Pp. 219-76. In English translation: *The Second Helvetic Confession.* In *The Book of Confessions.* New York: The United Presbyterian Church in the U.S.A., 1970.

CO *Ioannis Calvini Opera Quae Supersunt Omni.* 59 vols. Ed. Wilhelm Baum, Eduard Cunitz, and Eduard Reuss. Brunswick and Berlin, 1863-1900.

Decades Heinrich Bullinger. *Sermonum Decades duae, de potissimis verae religionis capitibus.* Zürich: Froschauer, 1549.
————. *Sermonum decas tertia.* Zürich: Froschauer, 1550.
————. *Sermonum decas quarta.* Zürich: Froschauer, 1550.
————. *Sermonum decas quinta.* Zürich: Froschauer, 1551.

HBBibl I *Heinrich Bullinger Werke,* pt. 1: *Bibliographie,* vol. 1: *Beschreibendes Verzeichnis der Gedruckten Werke von Heinrich Bullinger.* Ed. Joachim Staedtke. Zürich: Theologischer Verlag, 1972.

HBBibl II *Heinrich Bullinger Werke,* pt. 1: *Bibliographie,* vol. 2: *Beschreibendes Verzeichnis der Literatur über Heinrich Bullinger.* Ed. Erland Herkenrath. Zürich: Theologischer Verlag, 1977.

Historiae Johann H. Hottinger. *Historiae Ecclesiasticae Novi Testamenti.* Vol. 8. Zürich, 1667.

PSD Heinrich Bullinger. *The Decades of Heinrich Bullinger.* Ed. Thomas Harding. 3 vols. Parker Society, Cambridge University, 1849-52.

Summa Heinrich Bullinger. *Summa Christenlicher Religion.* Zürich: Froschauer, 1556. In Latin translation: *Compendium christianae religionis.* Zürich: Froschauer, 1556.

1

Bullinger—Author of "the Other Reformed Tradition"?

In older surveys of the history of doctrinal development during the Reformation, the reforming labor and theological contributions of many important figures were frequently overlooked. Among the magisterial Reformers, the names of Martin Luther, Ulrich Zwingli and John Calvin stood out. Many of their contemporaries in the reformatory movement of the sixteenth century, however, were neglected. Though this feature of the study of the Reformation may be understandable—certainly the aforementioned Reformers were leading figures not only in the sixteenth century but also in the development of the doctrinal traditions, respectively, of the Lutheran and Reformed churches—it often occurred at the cost of recognizing the significant contributions of others. Furthermore, by isolating a few leading Reformers among the many figures of prominence during the Protestant Reformation, Reformation studies risked over-simplifying the doctrinal ferment that marked this period. Figures whose theological writings were of great significance for the development of Reformation theology were sometimes given short shrift.

Heinrich Bullinger, successor to Ulrich Zwingli in Zürich, Switzerland, represents a notable instance of this neglect in older studies of the Reformation. In these studies, Bullinger often stood in the shadow of Zwingli, as though he were a figure of less importance to the development of the Reformation in Switzerland and the Rhineland.[1] Compared to the larger-than-life figure of Calvin, Bullinger's role in the reformational developments of the sixteenth century was often treated as though it was relatively negligible. Only in more recent studies has the prodigious labor

---

1. Cf. Edward A. Dowey, "Heinrich Bullinger's Theology: Thematic, Comprehensive, Schematic," in *Calvin Studies V: Presented at a Colloquium on Calvin Studies at Davidson College and Davidson College Presbyterian Church*, ed. John H. Leith (Jan. 19-20, 1990), 42: "Always he has borne the sobriquet 'Zwingli's successor,' and this has frequently been the point of departure for study of his work."

and theological contribution of Bullinger been more adequately acknowledged. Students of Bullinger's life and theology have demonstrated that Bullinger played an extraordinary role in the development of the Reformed tradition.[2] Though no comprehensive treatment of his theological viewpoint has yet been written, a number of important studies of various aspects of his thought and reformatory labor have, in significant measure, redressed the relative neglect of his work in older studies.[3]

However, with the more recent attention to the distinctive contribution of Bullinger as a key figure in the ecclesiastical and doctrinal development of the Reformation, a lively debate has ensued regarding Bullinger's role in the subsequent development of the Reformed tradition. Similar to the debates respecting the relation between Calvin and the Calvinists, or between the early Reformation and later Reformed scholasticism, students of Bullinger's reforming labor differ widely in their assessment of his influence upon the doctrinal developments of the late sixteenth and seventeenth centuries.

Nowhere has the debate regarding Bullinger's particular contributions to the history of the Reformed tradition been more vigorous than with respect to his doctrine of predestination. Though it is generally acknowledged that the doctrine of

2. Cf., for example, the following remark by J. Wayne Baker, *Heinrich Bullinger and the Covenant: The Other Reformed Tradition* (Athens, Ohio: Ohio University Press, 1980), xi: "Heinrich Bullinger was one of the makers of the Reformed tradition. It was Bullinger who preserved the Swiss Reformation after the death of Zwingli, and it was he who assured the essential unity of Reformed Protestantism with the First and Second Helvetic Confessions. During his forty-five-year tenure as leader of the Zürich church his importance in Reformed circles was unsurpassed, except perhaps by Calvin." For a comprehensive treatment of Bullinger's life and work, the outstanding sources remain Carl Pestalozzi, *Heinrich Bullinger: Leben und ausgewählte Schriften* (Elberfeld: R. L. Friderichs, 1858); Fritz Blanke, *Der junge Bullinger 1504-1531* (Zürich: Zwingli Verlag, 1942); and Heinrich Bullinger, *Heinrich Bullingers DIARIUM [Annales vitae] der Jahre 1504-1574. Zum 400. Geburtstag Bullingers am 18. Juli* 1904, ed. Emil Egli (Basel: Basler Buch-und Antiquariatshandlung vormals Adolf Geering, 1904). Brief sketches of Bullinger's life and labor are given by Baker, *Heinrich Bullinger and the Covenant*, xi-xxvi; and David C. Steinmetz, "Heinrich Bullinger (1504-1575): Covenant and the Continuity of Salvation History," in *Reformers in the Wings* (1971; reprint, Grand Rapids: Baker, 1981), 133-42.

3. For recent summaries of the study of Bullinger's work and theology, including the ongoing project to produce a complete critical edition of his works, see Fritz Büsser, *Wurzeln der Reformation in Zürich: Zum 500. Geburtstag des Reformators Huldrych Zwingli* (Leiden: E. J. Brill, 1985), 106-98; and Fritz Blanke and Immanuel Leuschner, *Heinrich Bullinger: Vater der reformierten Kirche* (Zürich: Theologischer Verlag, 1990). As will be evident from the secondary literature cited in this study, book-length treatments of Bullinger's theology typically address one or another aspect of his thought.

predestination was a key theological idiom for the Reformed tradition's exposition of the theme of *sola gratia*—salvation by grace alone through the work of the Redeemer—significant questions have been raised regarding Bullinger's understanding of this doctrine. Assessments of Bullinger's doctrine range from those which place his position squarely in the mainstream of the early Reformed tradition to those which argue that he demurred substantially from the position of Calvin and the tradition. Some interpreters have argued that, for Bullinger, the doctrine of predestination was largely displaced by the doctrine of the covenant. Thus, in the context of these assessments, the doctrine of predestination has become a focal point for the evaluation of Bullinger's contribution to the development of the Reformed tradition.

Though this study does not purport to be a complete exposition of Bullinger's doctrine of predestination, it aims to consider Bullinger's doctrine of predestination *in terms of this debate, particularly so far as it raises the question whether Bullinger's theology represents a substantial theological alternative to that associated with the name of Calvin.* Admittedly, a comprehensive study of Bullinger's doctrine of predestination has already been written.[4] However, what is needed is a study of Bullinger's doctrine of predestination within the framework of the ongoing assessment of his distinctive theological viewpoint. This study hopes to answer to this need.

The debate regarding Bullinger's doctrine of predestination has a complicated history in the older and in the more recent literature on Bullinger's theology. Because the discussion regarding Bullinger's understanding of predestination constitutes a window upon the larger field of Bullinger studies—particularly on the questions of Bullinger's uniqueness as a Reformed theologian and distinctive contribution to the development of the Reformed tradition—a study of Bullinger's doctrine of predestination faces the daunting challenge of finding its way through the thicket of previous studies.

In somewhat schematic form, the literature on Bullinger's doctrine of predestination can be divided into two broad periods. In the first period of older studies, the emphasis was upon a comparison of Bullinger's doctrine with that of Calvin. In these studies, the primary question that surfaced was—did Bullinger agree substantially with Calvin's understanding of election? Or were there significant differences between Calvin and Bullinger

---

4. Peter Walser, *Die Prädestination bei Heinrich Bullinger im Zusammenhang mit seiner Gotteslehre* (Zürich: Zwingli Verlag, 1957).

that remained throughout the course of their theological development and writings? In the second period of more recent studies, there has been a subtle shift in emphasis. Rather than simply evaluating Bullinger's doctrine by the standard of Calvin's teaching, students of Bullinger's thought have increasingly posited a significant difference between Calvin, the theologian of predestination, and Bullinger, the theologian of the covenant. In these more recent studies, interpreters have increasingly argued that Bullinger should be regarded as a theologian in his own right, and that his theology is distinguished by its emphasis upon the covenant rather than election.

In order to provide a context for the following study of Bullinger's doctrine of predestination, then, we will begin with a review of these two successive periods in the history of Bullinger studies. Because these studies have also been influenced by an ongoing debate regarding the proper interpretation of Calvin's theology, this review will include a brief excursus on this debate.

A. The Older Literature: Comparing Bullinger and Calvin on Predestination

In the older literature on Bullinger's theology, the principal question respecting his doctrine of predestination concerns its compatibility with that of Calvin. This question is often further refined in terms of the issue whether there was a change in Bullinger's view, especially between the years 1551 and 1566, in the direction of a more "Calvinistic" understanding. Did Bullinger move from an earlier, moderate conception of predestination to a later, more "Calvinistic" one?[5] Or did Bullinger maintain throughout his life a distinctive understanding of this doctrine?

The dominance of the issue of Bullinger's agreement with Calvin on the doctrine of predestination in this earlier period of Bullinger studies can be readily documented. On the one hand, a number of interpreters argue for the basic compatibility of their views;[6] and on the other, a number of interpreters argue for their

---

5. I am placing the adjective in quotation marks because what is meant by a "Calvinistic" doctrine of predestination is itself the subject of considerable dispute. I will summarize in the following section what many of these writers understand by a "Calvinistic" doctrine.

6. See, for example, Fritz Blanke, "Entsehung und Bedeutung des Zweiten Helvetischen Bekenntnisses," in *400 Jahre Zweites Helvetisches Bekenntnis* (Zürich/Stuttgart: Zwingli Verlag, 1966), 13-25; W. Kolfhaus, "Der Verkehr Calvins mit Bullinger," in *Festschrift zum 400. Geburtstage Johann Calvins: Calvinstudien*, ed. Bohatec (Leipzig: Verlag von Rudolph Haupt, 1909), 27-125; Otto Ritschl, *Die reformierte Theologie des 16. Und des 17. Jahrhunderts in ihrer Entstehung und Entwicklung, Orthodoxie und Synkretismus in der*

20

incompatibility.[7] On the first interpretation—among those who treat Bullinger's view as compatible with that of Calvin—a difference of emphasis may be discerned between those who suggest that Bullinger's approach to predestination was more practical and pastoral in character than Calvin's,[8] and those who suggest that the two were in complete accord both in their approach to and position on this doctrine.[9] Among these interpreters, those who emphasize the pastoral character of Bullinger's doctrine detect no significant change in his writings on the doctrine. However, those who argue that Bullinger's position was in complete agreement with Calvin's, often claim that Bullinger altered his position on predestination from an earlier, moderate view to a later, more "Calvinistic" one. Joachim Staedtke, one advocate of this claim, links the shift in Bullinger's view with the Zürich conflict over predestination in 1560, the date

altprotestantischen Theologie (Göttingen: Vandenhoeck & Ruprecht, 1926), vol. 3; Gottfried Locher, "Bullinger und Calvin—Probleme des Vergleichs ihrer Theologien," in *Heinrich Bullinger, 1504-1575, Gesammelte Aufsätze zum 400 Todestag,* ed. U. Gäbler & Erland Herkenrath, *Zürcher Beiträge Zur Reformationsgeschichte* (Zürich: Theologischer Verlag, 1975), vol. 8, 1-33; Emil Egli, "Zur Erinnerung an Zwinglis Nachfolger Heinrich Bullinger," *Zwingliana* 1 (1904): 419-50; Joachim Staedtke, "Der Zürcher Prädestinationsstreit von 1560," *Zwingliana* 9 (1953): 536-46; and A. Schweizer, *Die Protestantischen Centraldogmen in Ihrer Entwicklung Innerhalb Der Reformierten Kirche, Erste Hälfte, Das 16. Jahrhundert* (Zürich: Orell, Füssli, 1854).

7. Hans Emil Weber, *Reformation, Orthodoxie und Rationalismus,* Erster Teil, *Von Der Reformation Zur Orthodoxie,* (1937-1951; reprint, Darmstadt: Wissenschaftliche Buchgesellschaft, 1966), Zweiter Halbband; Antonius Johannes Van't Hooft, *De Theologie van Heinrich Bullinger in betrekking tot de Nederlandse Reformatie* (Amsterdam: Is. De Hoogh, 1888); M. A. Gooszen, *Heinrich Bullinger en de strijd over de Praedestinatie* (Rotterdam, 1909); Ernst Koch, *Die Theologie der Confessio Helvetica Posterior* (Neukirchen: Verlag Des Erziehungsvereins, 1968), 103-15; Walter Hollweg, *Heinrich Bullingers Hausbuch: Eine Untersuchung über die Anfänge der reformierten Predigtliteratur* (Neukirchen: Verlag der Buchhandlung des Erziehungsvereins, 1956); Gottfried Adam, *Der Streit um die Prädestination im ausgehenden 16. Jahrhundert* (Neukirchener Verlag, 1970); and, with some ambivalence, Peter Walser, *Die Prädestination bei Heinrich Bullinger.*

8. Blanke, *Der junge Bullinger,* 18: "Bullinger lehnt in Hinblick auf die praedestinatio jegliches Theoretisieren ab und gibt der Lehre von der doppelten Vorherbestimmung eine Wendung ins Existenzielle. Doppelte Prädestination, das bedeutet für den einzelnen praktisch: Entscheide dich für Christus! Das Prädestinationsdogma bekommt also bei Bullinger einen seelsorgerlichen (pastoralen) Charakter." See Kolfhaus, "Der Verkehr Calvins mit Bullinger," 83-84; O. Ritschl, *Die reformierte Theologie,* 248; Locher, "Bullinger und Calvin," 24; and Egli, "Zur Erinnerung an Zwinglis Nachfolger Heinrich Bullinger," 425.

9. Staedtke, "Der Zürcher Prädestinationsstreit von 1560," 536; Schweizer, *Die Protestantischen Centraldogmen,* 285ff.

of Bibliander's retirement from the Zürich Academy.[10] However, Alexander Schweizer, the most forceful exponent of this approach, sees a shift in Bullinger's view under the influence of Peter Martyr Vermigli and cites as evidence Bullinger's agreement with the Zürich *Gutachten* of Dec. 29, 1561.[11]

On the second interpretation—among those who claim that Bullinger's view is incompatible with that of Calvin—Bullinger's doctrine of predestination is treated as a subject of independent interest for students of the history of doctrine. While those who follow this interpretation do so for varying reasons, they commonly claim that Bullinger's view was neither that of Calvin nor that of later Reformed orthodoxy, but that it represented a distinctive contribution within the sphere of early Reformed debate regarding the doctrine of predestination.[12] Some aspects of Bullinger's view which are adduced in support of this claim are his alleged rejection of a double decree,[13] his emphasis upon the universal promise of salvation,[14] and his orientation to the doctrine of the covenant rather than the decree of God.[15] However these emphases

10. Staedtke, "Der Zürcher Prädestinationsstreit von 1560," 536: "In Zürich hat der dogmengeschichtliche Übergang von einer stark gemilderten Erwählungstheologie zur strengen Prädestinationslehre Calvins seine historische Kennzeichnung durch die Entlassung Theodor Biblianders erfahren." I shall treat this conflict of 1560 in Chapter 4 below.

11. Schweizer, *Die Protestantischen Centraldogmen*, 285ff. and 459. I shall also consider the influence of Vermigli and the significance of Bullinger's concurrence with these *Gutachten* in Chapter 4.

12. The following comment of Ernst Koch, *Die Theologie der Confessio Helvetica Posterior*, 104, is fairly representative of this approach: "Aber Bullinger von Calvin her verstehen oder an Calvin messen zu wollen wäre keine sachgemässe Methode, ihm gerecht zu werden. Man wird vielmehr festhalten müssen, dass Bullinger eine eigenständige, tief in seiner Gesamttheologie verwurzelte Konzeption seiner Prädestinationslehre vorgelegt hat."

13. Weber, *Reformation, Orthodoxie und Rationalismus*, 92; Van't Hooft, *De Theologie van Heinrich Bullinger*, 62; Hollweg, *Heinrich Bullinger's Hausbuch*, 338.

14. Weber, *Reformation, Orthodoxie und Rationalismus*, 92; Van't Hooft, *De Theologie van Heinrich Bullinger*, 72-73, 84-85. Van't Hooft cites the Second Helvetic Confession in support of his position, and also points to the appeal that the Remonstrants made at Dort to Bullinger as evidence for distinguishing Bullinger's view from that of Calvin. Koch, *Die Theologie der Confessio Helvetica Posterior*, 95, and Walser, *Die Prädestination bei Heinrich Bullinger*, 149, however, both argue against attributing universalism too quickly to Bullinger.

15. Van't Hooft, *De Theologie van Heinrich Bullinger*, 72ff. Cf. Gottlob Schrenk, *Gottesreich und Bund im älteren Protestantismus vornehmlich bei Johannes Coccejus, zugleich ein Beitrag zur Geschichte des Pietismus und der heilsgeschichtlichen Theologie* (1923; reprint, Darmstadt: Wissenschaftliche Buchgesellschaft, 1967), 40-44. Schrenk suggests that Bullinger treats the doctrine of the covenant rather than predestination as a constitutive dogmatic

are interpreted, they suggest, when coupled with other historical evidence,[16] that Bullinger differed significantly in his view from Calvin.

Both of these interpretations, then, are important for our purpose, as they illustrate the need for an examination of Bullinger's doctrine of predestination, including the question whether there was a development in his thinking from his earlier to his later writings. For all of these interpreters, the question of the uniqueness of Bullinger's view in comparison to that of Calvin is paramount. The first interpretation, which argues for the compatibility of their views, claims either that Bullinger was *consistent* throughout his life in espousing a moderate doctrine of election or that he *altered* his position to bring it into complete accord with Calvin as well as later Reformed orthodoxy. For those who adopt the second interpretation, which argues for the incompatibility of their views, it is commonly claimed that Bullinger *consistently* held to an independent point of view.

B. The Debate Regarding Calvin's Doctrine of Predestination

One of the serious complications in the study of Bullinger's doctrine of predestination, especially in the older literature, is its dependence upon prior assumptions regarding Calvin's doctrine. Interpreters of this period typically argue that a "Calvinistic" doctrine of predestination included all of the following elements: (1) a doctrine of double predestination; (2) an explicitly developed doctrine of God's pre-temporal decree; (3) the inclusion, in some manner, of the fall into sin within the scope of God's sovereign purposes; and (4) a general tendency to draw logical conclusions in treating the Scriptural references to predestination and election. Though some of these interpreters are hesitant regarding elements "(2)" and "(4)"—so far, at least, as they express the idea that Calvin's theology was the product of a rigid predestinarianism or

principle, which accounts for the "universal tendency" of his thought. However, he acknowledges that the question of the relation between Bullinger's doctrines of the covenant and predestination requires further exploration. As we shall see in what follows, this suggestion has found a more firm footing in some more recent studies of Bullinger's theology.

16. Adam, *Die Streit um die Prädestination*, 85, notes that the Reformed theologian, Huber, appealed to Bullinger against Calvin and Beza in the Berne predestination conflict of 1588. He also notes that the Synod of Dordtrecht implicitly acknowledged Bullinger's distinctive view when it attempted to interpret him as a "Calvinist" on the basis of his participation in the Zanchius-Marbach dispute of 1561.

"metaphysic of the divine will," all of its elements deduced in descending order from this central principle—many of them, most notably Alexander Schweizer and Hans Emil Weber, argue from this point of view.

However, more recent studies of Calvin's doctrine of predestination exhibit a considerable diversity of opinion regarding his view. No doubt Calvin's doctrine of predestination included some of these elements, e.g., a double decree of election and reprobation, an express formulation of God's pre-temporal decree/s, and the inclusion of the fall into sin within the scope of God's will. But that his theology may be characterized as a deductivistic system, derived from a "central dogma" of pre-destinarianism, has been challenged by many recent competent studies of Calvin's doctrine.

Though it is not my purpose here to sort out the complexities of the interpretation of Calvin's doctrine of predestination, a brief excursus on three major approaches in the literature will help to illumine the ongoing debate respecting the compatibility of Calvin and Bullinger's views.

First, in the nineteenth century, an older approach argued that the "central dogma" of the Reformed tradition—authored and identified with the name of Calvin—was the doctrine of predestination. In this school of thought, Reformed theology from Calvin to later orthodoxy was regarded as an all-embracing system, logically deduced from the principle of God's sovereign, predestinating will. All of the doctrinal *loci* of Reformed theology find their origin and basis, accordingly, in this first principle of thought.[17] One often overlooked feature of this school of interpretation is the diverse theological interests that it served. For Alexander Schweizer, the development of a predestinarian system was a positive one, lending support to his own Schleiermacherian system of theology. For Heinrich Heppe, the Reformed system of predestination compared unfavorably to the nonpredestinarian, largely Melanchthonian, German theology. And for Hans Emil Weber, the predestinarianism of the Reformed tradition compared unfavorably to the (Lutheran) Reformation's prior and basic

17. For a representation of this older school of thought, see Alexander Schweizer, *Die protestantischen Centraldogmen*; Heinrich Heppe, *Die Dogmatik der evangelisch-reformierten Kirche*, Neu durchgesehen und herausgegeben von Ernst Bizer (Neukirchen: Moers, 1935): in translation, *Reformed Dogmatics Set Out and Illustrated from the Sources*, rev. and ed. Ernst Bizer, trans. G. T. Thomson (1950; reprint, Grand Rapids: Baker, 1978); and Hans Emil Weber, *Reformation, Orthodoxie und Rationalismus*.

commitment to justification as the article by which the church stands or falls.

Second, in the twentieth century, largely under the influence of Karl Barth and neo-orthodox theology, a second approach has argued for a substantial divergence and discontinuity between Calvin's theology and that of later Reformed orthodoxy. Whereas Calvin's theology was Christocentric and non-rationalistic, the theology of later Reformed orthodoxy recast Reformed theology into a predestinarian (decretal) and rationalistic system. Unlike the first school of thought that emphasizes *continuity* in the relation between Calvin and later Reformed orthodoxy, this school emphasizes *discontinuity* and gave rise to a tradition of scholarship that pitted Calvin against the "Calvinists" and took a severely critical view of the tradition of orthodoxy. Interpreters of this school often argue that Theodore Beza was responsible for this declension from Calvin's Christocentric theology into a rationalistic theology of the divine decree.[18]

Finally, in more recent studies of Calvin's doctrine and its relation to subsequent developments in the Reformed tradition, a third approach, represented by the work of Richard Muller, has rejected the "central dogma" claim and the exaggerated stress upon discontinuity between Calvin and later Reformed orthodoxy. According to this school of interpretation, there are significant continuities not only between the Patristic and Medieval exegetical and theological traditions and those of the Reformation era, but also between the Reformation and post-Reformation developments within the Reformed tradition. Neither in Calvin nor in the theologies of the orthodox theologians of the late sixteenth and seventeenth centuries do we find a theological system that is rigidly deductivistic or derivative of the doctrine of the divine

---

18. For examples of this tendency in the interpretation of Calvin's doctrine of predestination, see Paul Jacobs, *Prädestination und Verantwortlichkeit bei Calvin* (Neukirchen, 1937); and Wilhelm Niesel, *Theology of Calvin*, trans. Harold Knight (1956; reprint, Grand Rapids: Baker, 1980). For the argument that posits a substantial discontinuity between Calvin and the Calvinists, see Basil Hall, "Calvin Against the Calvinists," in *John Calvin: A Collection of Distinguished Essays*, ed. Gervase Duffield (Grand Rapids: Eerdmans, 1966), 19-37; R. T. Kendall, *Calvin and Calvinism to 1649* (New York and London: Oxford University Press, 1978); and Charles S. McCoy, "Johannes Cocceius: Federal Theologian," *Scottish Journal of Theology* 16 (1963): 354, 364-69. For a representation of the claim that Reformed orthodoxy introduced a scholastic deductivism into the Reformed tradition, at odds with Calvin's Christocentricism, see Brian Armstrong, *Calvinism and the Amyraut Heresy: Protestant Scholasticism and Humanism in Seventeenth Century France* (Madison: University of Wisconsin Press, 1969); and Ernst Bizer, *Frühorthodoxie und Rationalismus* (Zürich: EVZ Verlag, 1963).

decrees. Though among the orthodox there is a recasting of Calvin and the Reformation's doctrine in a scholastic *form*, there is a substantial body of continuity in doctrinal content between them.[19]

Though it is not my purpose in this brief excursus to resolve the issues this scholarship raises, my sympathies lie largely with this third school. Calvin's doctrine of election, though an integral aspect of his theology of the knowledge of the Triune God as Creator and Redeemer, is not an abstract first principle. Nor is it the metaphysical basis for a deductivistic system (*contra* the first approach). But neither is Calvin's doctrine a sixteenth century anticipation of Barth's Christocentrism, in relation to which the theology of the orthodox was a serious declension (*contra* the second approach). Within the world of Calvin's biblical and confessional theology, the doctrine of election has an important place, emphasizing in the most dramatic way the themes of *solo Christo* and *sola fide*. But it remains subordinate to the living center of Calvin's thinking: the sovereign initiatives and accomplishments of the Triune God in creation and redemption.[20]

This debate regarding Calvin's doctrine of predestination complicates any attempt to compare his doctrine with that of Bullinger. As we shall see in the course of this study, assumptions about Calvin's doctrine often shape the way his view is compared or contrasted with that of Bullinger.

19. See, for example, Richard Muller, *Christ and the Decree: Christology and Predestination in Reformed Theology from Calvin to Perkins* (1986; reprint, Grand Rapids: Baker, 1988); idem, *Post-Reformation Reformed Dogmatics: II. Holy Scripture: the Cognitive Foundation of Theology* (Grand Rapids: Baker, 1993), 7-11, 52-63, 88-94, 181-83, 240-48; idem, "Calvin and the 'Calvinists': Assessing Continuities and Discontinuities Between the Reformation and Orthodoxy, Part One," *Calvin Theological Journal* 30/2 (Nov., 1995): 345-75; idem, "The Myth of 'Decretal Theology,'" *Calvin Theological Journal* 30/1 (April, 1995): 159-67; and idem, "Calvin and the 'Calvinists,' Part Two," *Calvin Theological Journal* 31/1 (April, 1996): 125-60. Muller's studies provide a comprehensive survey of these schools of interpretation and their extensive literature. My summary provides only a sampling of sources and represents, admittedly, something of a simplification of his analyses.

20. Cf. Cornelis P. Venema, *The Twofold Nature of the Gospel in Calvin's Theology: The* duplex gratia dei *and the Interpretation of Calvin's Theology* (Ph.D. diss., Princeton Theological Seminary, 1985), 286-87: "The point of departure for the whole of Calvin's theological reflection is Trinitarian and Christological.... Though there is a genuine sense in which his theology may be termed 'Christocentric,' a theology of revelation and redemption in Christ, this redemptive concentration does not bespeak a 'Christomonism' wherein the whole economy of the Triune God's creative and redemptive action loses its theological importance."

C. More Recent Literature: Bullinger as Covenant Theologian

In the period of more recent studies of Bullinger's theology, the focus of debate regarding his doctrine of predestination has shifted. Whereas the older studies focussed upon the question of Bullinger's similarity or dissimilarity with Calvin, the newer studies have emphasized Bullinger's *independence* as a covenant theologian. Though these studies retain an interest in the question of the extent of Bullinger's agreement or disagreement with Calvin's theology, they start from the premise that Bullinger was preeminently a theologian of the covenant and therefore differed substantially from Calvin on the subject of predestination. Calvin was a theologian of predestination, whose covenant doctrine was controlled and determined by his doctrine of the divine decrees. Bullinger, by contrast, was a theologian of the covenant, whose predestination doctrine was controlled and determined by his doctrine of the divine covenantal purposes in history. What these studies add to the older contention that Bullinger differed from Calvin on the doctrine of predestination, then, is the claim that this difference was the product of a substantially different theological orientation. Because Bullinger was a theologian of the covenant, he authored (or contributed to the formation of) a distinctive Reformed theological tradition oriented to God's covenant working in history rather than to his pre-temporal decree.[21]

Undoubtedly, the most vigorous exponent today of this interpretation of Bullinger is J. Wayne Baker.[22] Baker's inter-

---

21. This is not to say that, among more recent studies, the older interest in directly comparing Calvin and Bullinger's doctrines of predestination has been eclipsed. For two recent defenses of the interpretation that regards predestination as a "central dogma" in Calvin and Bullinger's thought, see Jürgen Moltmann, *Prädestination und Perseveranz: Geschichte und Bedeutung der reformierten Lehre "de perseverantia sanctorum"* (Neukirchen: Verlag der Buchhandlung des Erziehungsvereins, 1961), 100-103; and John Patrick Donnelly, *Calvinism and Scholasticism in Vermigli's Doctrine of Grace* (Leiden: E. J. Brill, 1976), 184. For an interpretation that detects some modest differences between Calvin and Bullinger on predestination, see Muller, *Christ and the Decree*, 39-47. For a defense of the full compatibility of their doctrines, see Peter Lillback, "The Continuing Conundrum: Calvin and the Conditionality of the Covenant," *Calvin Theological Journal* 29/1 (April, 1994): 58-74. My language of "two periods" in the history of research is schematic.

22. See J. Wayne Baker, *Heinrich Bullinger and the Covenant*, 27-54, 193-98, *et passim*; J. Wayne Baker with Charles S. McCoy, *Fountainhead of Federalism: Heinrich Bullinger and the Covenantal Tradition, with a translation of* De testamento seu foedere Dei unio et aeterno (1534) (Louisville, KY: Westminster/John Knox Press, 1991); and J. Wayne Baker, "Heinrich Bullinger,

pretation, however, stands in a historical line with other studies of the emergence and development of the doctrine of the covenant in the Reformed tradition.[23]

Interest in the history of the doctrine of the covenant in the Reformed tradition was stimulated significantly by the ground-breaking work of Perry Miller. In his "The Marrow of Puritan Divinity"[24] and first volume of *The New England Mind*,[25] Miller argued that the doctrine of the covenant was central to the tradition of seventeenth century Puritanism. Unlike the rigid predestinarianism that characterized Calvin's thought, the Puritans' view of the covenant represented a significant modification within Reformed theology, a modification oriented more to God's redemptive purpose in history than to the divine decree. According to Miller, Calvin "hardly made any mention of the covenant"[26] by contrast to the Puritans for whom it was a controlling interest.

Miller's claim not surprisingly stimulated a number of studies which investigated the origins or sources for the Puritans' covenant doctrine. Among the first and most formative of these was Leonard J. Trinterud's "The Origins of Puritanism,"[27] in which Trinterud maintained that the Puritans' covenant idea derived from the influence of the Reformed tradition in Zürich and the Rhineland, and not from Calvin. Though Trinterud—contrary to Miller's earlier claim that Calvin hardly mentioned the covenant—recognized the importance of the covenant in Calvin's theology, he posited a substantial difference in covenant doctrine between

the Covenant, and the Reformed Tradition in Retrospect," *Sixteenth Century Journal* 29/2 (Summer, 1998): 359-76.

23. For a sketch and critical evaluation of this line of interpretation, see Lyle D. Bierma, "Federal Theology in the Sixteenth Century: Two Traditions," *Westminster Theological Journal* 44/2 (Fall, 1983): 304-21; and Peter Lillback, "The Continuing Conundrum: Calvin and the Conditionality of the Covenant," 42-74.

24. In *Errand into the Wilderness* (New York: Harper Torchbacks, 1964), 48-98.

25. *The New England Mind: The Seventeenth Century* (New York: MacMillan, 1939).

26. "The Marrow of Puritan Divinity," 57. For a critical examination of Miller's study, see George M. Marsden, "Perry Miller's Rehabilitation of the Puritans: A Critique," *Church History* 39 (1970): 99-104.

27. *Church History* 20 (1951): 37-57. Miller's and Trinterud's studies, together with those we consider below, are not primarily interested in the doctrinal or theological aspects of the covenant, but in the impact of the covenant idea upon developments in English and American federal political philosophy and social contract theories. My interest, on the contrary, is primarily with the doctrinal or theological issues so far as they relate to Bullinger's doctrine of predestination.

Calvin and Geneva on the one hand, and the Rhineland Reformers and Zürich on the other. In the course of his study, Trinterud elaborated this difference by means of a series of contrasts: whereas Calvin taught a *unilateral covenant,* the Zürich/Rhineland Reformers taught a *bilateral covenant;* whereas Calvin taught an *unconditional covenant promise,* the Zürich/Rhineland Reformers taught a *conditional covenant promise;* whereas Calvin placed the burden of fulfilling the covenant upon *God's work,* the Zürich/Rhineland Reformers placed the burden upon *human responsibility;* and whereas Calvin located the fulfillment of the covenant in *the person and work of Christ,* the Zürich/Rhineland Reformers located the fulfillment of the covenant *in the faithful obedience* of those with whom God covenanted.[28]

For the purposes of this study, it is not necessary to trace the influence of Trinterud's thesis—the positing of two radically different covenant traditions, the Genevan and the Rhineland—upon study of the origins and character of the covenant theology of the Puritans.[29] What interests us is the way in which this "two covenant traditions" thesis has been embraced and vigorously defended by J. Wayne Baker and Charles S. McCoy in their recent interpretation of Bullinger's theology. For the defense of the validity of this thesis in the interpretation of Bullinger's theology has far-reaching implications for a proper understanding of his doctrine of predestination.

J. Wayne Baker, in his study, *Heinrich Bullinger and the Covenant: The Other Reformed Tradition,* has offered an extensive defense of the "two covenant traditions" thesis. As the single most comprehensive study of Bullinger's theological viewpoint in the English language, Baker's work represents an important point of reference in Bullinger studies. Coupled with a subsequent work, coauthored by Charles S. McCoy, *Fountainhead of Federalism: Heinrich Bullinger and the Covenantal Tradition,* Baker has provided a vigorous defense of the Trinterud thesis that the covenant tradition in Puritan thought stems from the influence of the Rhineland Reformers, and Bullinger in particular, rather than Calvin. He has also added his voice to those who posit an insuperable difference in doctrine between the Reformed tradition stemming from Calvin, in which predestination is the governing

28. "The Origins of Puritanism," 44-45, 56 fn27. These contrasts represent Bierma's summary of Trinterud's argument.

29. For a brief sketch of this influence, see Bierma, "Federal Theology in the Sixteenth Century," 306-9.

theological idea, and the other Reformed tradition stemming from the Rhineland, in which covenant is the predominant theme.

In a recent defense of his interpretation of Bullinger as a covenant theologian and author of "the other Reformed tradition," Baker summarizes his position in four theses: (1) the doctrine of the covenant is the central organizing principle of Bullinger's theology; (2) Bullinger taught a "bilateral, conditional" covenant, contrary to Calvin's unilateral, unconditional testamentary doctrine of the covenant; (3) consistent with his emphasis upon the conditionality of the covenant, Bullinger taught "a moderate, single predestination in contrast to Calvin's double predestination"; and (4) Bullinger's covenant doctrine represents the original Reformed tradition, in comparison to which the doctrine of Calvin and the Calvinists represents a "later alternative in the matter of the covenant and predestination."[30] These theses are sweeping in their claims and constitute a formidable challenge to any interpretation that would argue a substantial compatibility or continuity between the theologies of covenant and of predestination, represented by Bullinger and Calvin, respectively.[31]

According to Baker, the doctrine of the covenant and the doctrine of predestination constitute two divergent ways of expressing the doctrine of salvation by grace alone:

> The vital Reformation doctrines of *sola fide* and *sola gratia* found two different modes of expression within early Reformed circles. The most prevalent was the Augustinian idea of testament, linked with an affirmation of double predestination, which found its classic statement in the writings of Calvin. The other Reformed tradition, existing alongside the more heavily predestinarian

30. Baker, "Heinrich Bullinger, the Covenant, and the Reformed Tradition in Retrospect," 359.

31. However, there are a number of good studies of Calvin's doctrine of the covenant that adduce compelling evidence against the claim that Calvin taught a unilateral (monopleuric) and unconditional testamentary view. These studies clearly show that Calvin taught a "conditional" covenant doctrine, though in a form that was closely correlated with his insistence upon God's gracious election. To echo an ancient formulation of Augustine, Calvin believed that *God gave his elect the faith he demanded from them in the gospel*; faith is both a divine gift and a human responsibility. See Bierma, "Federal Theology in the Sixteenth Century," 313-16; Anthony A. Hoekema, "Calvin's Doctrine of the Covenant of Grace," *The Reformed Review* 15 (1962): 1-12; idem, "The Covenant of Grace in Calvin's Teaching," *Calvin Theological Journal* 2 (1967): 133-61; Peter Lillback, *The Binding of God: Calvin's Role in the Development of Covenant Theology* (Grand Rapids: Baker, 2001), 176-209, 214-41, *et passim*; and idem, "The Continuing Conundrum," 42-74.

Calvinist tradition, was Bullinger's notion of conditional covenant.[32]

Whereas the Augustinian/Calvinian doctrine of testament is the "logical corollary of an absolute predestinarian stance," including the doctrine of a double decree of election and reprobation, Bullinger's doctrine of the covenant found its corollary in a "more moderate single or even a conditional predestinarian teaching."[33] The chief emphases in Bullinger's moderate doctrine of predestination are "God's election of those who believe . . . in, through, and for Christ," and salvation "totally of God's free grace."[34] Though Bullinger consistently rejected synergism with its affirmation of the freedom of the will in relation to the call of the gospel, he nonetheless taught a kind of "universalism" both in terms of the call of the gospel and the provisions of Christ's atoning work for all. Those whom God elects are those who believe in response to the gospel; those whom God rejects are those who willfully and culpably disbelieve. In Bullinger's understanding of predestination, any doctrine of reprobation would inevitably shift the blame for unbelief from the sinner to God himself. It would also undermine the universal call and promise of the gospel to all.[35] Describing Bullinger's doctrine, Baker asserts, "Men did not refuse salvation because God foreknew their refusal; rather God foreknew their refusal because they would refuse. Thus there was foreknowledge without predestination, in the case of those who would refuse salvation; but those whom God predestined would have faith because of His election."[36]

32. *Heinrich Bullinger and the Covenant*, 27.

33. *Heinrich Bullinger and the Covenant*, 28. Baker's use of the expression "conditional predestinarian" is ambiguous. It is not clear whether he means to say that Bullinger taught a doctrine of election upon the condition of (foreseen) faith, or a doctrine that merely correlates the assurance of election with the act of faith in Christ, an act that is a gift of God's free grace.

34. *Heinrich Bullinger and the Covenant*, 29.

35. *Heinrich Bullinger and the Covenant*, 29-30.

36. *Heinrich Bullinger and the Covenant*, 30. According to Baker, this summarizes Bullinger's teaching in his *Oratio* of 1536 on predestination and other matters, a teaching to which he held consistently throughout his writings. We will have occasion to consider this *Oratio* in Chapter 2 below. The ambiguity mentioned in fn33 above is evident in Baker's language: on the one hand, he acknowledges that Bullinger taught a doctrine of *unconditional* election (the elect believe not so as to become elect but because they are elect, faith being God's gracious gift); on the other, he argues that what distinguishes the elect and nonelect is their respective responses of believing and disbelieving (as conditions for salvation or damnation).

What Baker and others have added to the older questions clustering around Bullinger's doctrine of predestination—e.g., Did Bullinger agree or disagree with Calvin's position? Was there a development in his doctrine from an earlier, moderate view to a later, more "Calvinistic" conception?—is the question of whether Bullinger's view differed widely from Calvin and the later Reformed tradition's doctrine because of the ruling interests of his covenant doctrine. The claims of Baker and others regarding "the other Reformed tradition" go far beyond anything asserted in the older studies of Bullinger's doctrine of predestination. Not only do they presume a definite idea of the governing place of predestination in Calvin's thought, including the idea that this was correlated with an unconditional, testamentary view of the covenant, but they also argue that Bullinger's theology of the covenant *radically shaped* his formulation of the doctrine of predestination. The typical elements that allegedly comprise Bullinger's doctrine—a single decree of election, the correlation of election with faith, an emphasis upon the universal call and provision of the gospel, the stress upon human responsibility in relation to the working of God's grace—are derived from the basic requirements of his covenant doctrine. Rather than being oriented theologically to the pretemporal decree of God, Bullinger focussed upon the administration of God's saving purposes in the history of the covenant of grace.

D. Procedure and Outline of This Study

Now that we have provided a survey of the rather extensive literature on Bullinger's doctrine of predestination, in its earlier and more recent periods, we are in a position to provide a prospectus of the procedure and outline of the following study.

The key questions relating to Bullinger's doctrine that emerge in this literature are readily apparent. In summary form, they are as follows: first, does Bullinger's doctrine represent a substantial alternative to that of Calvin?; second, if Bullinger's most important treatments of the doctrine of predestination are considered in their historical order, from earlier to later, do they reflect any significant change in his understanding from an earlier, more moderate position to a later, more fully developed and Calvinistic position?; and third, is there an intimate correlation between Bullinger's doctrine of the covenant and predestination which leads Bullinger to articulate the kind of "conditional" predestinarianism suggested by Baker and others?

In the following chapters, these questions will form the background to our treatment of Bullinger's writings on the doctrine of predestination throughout the course of his reforming labor. This treatment will proceed in the following order: in the next chapter, we will consider three of Bullinger's more comprehensive treatments of the doctrine of predestination in the period from 1536 to 1556; Chapter 3 will offer a survey and analysis of Bullinger's correspondence on predestination during the years 1551-1553, particularly his correspondence with Calvin in the Bolsec controversy, and then with Traheron; Chapter 4 will analyze and interpret the retirement of Bibliander from the Zürich Academy in 1560, and the Zürich *Gutachten* of 1561; and Chapter 5 will offer a treatment of the Second Helvetic Confession in terms of its importance for the questions at issue. Only after having traced the articulation of Bullinger's doctrine of predestination in the historical sequence of his more important writings on the subject, will we be in a position to answer the questions raised in previous studies of Bullinger's thought.

2

Bullinger's Doctrine of Predestination, 1536-1556

A commonplace in studies of Bullinger's writings is the observation that his works typically have an occasional and pastoral quality. In the extensive corpus of Bullinger's writings, there is nothing to compare, for example, with Calvin's *Institutio* or Melanchthon's *Loci Communes*.[1] Though Bullinger produced several important statements of Reformed doctrine, none of them can be simply regarded as *the* definitive or comprehensive summary of his thought.[2] Students of Bullinger's life and thought are, therefore, primarily dependent upon several occasional, as well as more comprehensive, writings to determine his position on the doctrine of predestination in the early and later stages of his work as the *Antistes* (chief pastor) of the church in Zürich after Zwingli's death in 1531. Determining Bullinger's position requires a consideration in historical sequence of a number of the more important instances in which he commented at length on the

1. Cf. David C. Steinmetz, "Heinrich Bullinger," 140: "Against the tendency to write systematic theological treatises by the *Loci* method, arranging all doctrines according to the logical categories of Aristotle, Bullinger helped to preserve within the Reformed tradition a homiletical approach to theology, in which biblical categories and history of salvation are more important organizing principles than the categories of Aristotle." Staedtke, *HBBibl I*, lists 772 entries, which includes all known translations and editions of Bullinger's works. Bullinger's unpublished writings number about 300. The ongoing project to publish Bullinger's writings is projected to come to circa 100 volumes. See *Heinrich Bullinger Werke*, pt. 2: *Briefwechsel*, ed. Ulrich Gäbler et al., vols. 1-7; pt. 3: *Theologische Schriften*, ed. Ulrich Gäbler et al., vols. 1-2 (Zürich: Theologischer Verlag, 1973-95).

2. However, Ernst Koch, *Die Theologie der Confessio Helvetica Posterior*, 415, maintains that Bullinger was a truly systematic thinker whose *Confessio Helvetica Posterior* is "ein dogmatisches Werk von grossartiger Geschlossenheit und imponierende theologischer Folgerichtigkeit." Koch maintains that the doctrine of the covenant is the central and organizing principle of Bullinger's system. Dowey, "Heinrich Bullinger as Theologian," 41-60, more persuasively maintains that Bullinger's writings fall into three main types—biblical commentary, thematic and polemic treatises, and comprehensive presentations—none of which qualifies as a full-fledged "systematic" work.

subject of predestination. It also requires some attention to the circumstances and occasion for his addressing the doctrine.

In the earlier period of Bullinger's reformatory activity in Zürich, there are at least three works that provide a comprehensive overview of his understanding of predestination.[3] These works antedate or, in one instance, coincide with his involvement in several controversies respecting the doctrine later in his life, an involvement which, as we previously noted, some interpreters believe led him to revise his thinking in the direction of a more rigorous viewpoint. The three documents of special significance in this first period of Bullinger's labor are: an *Oratio* in 1536 on predestination and other matters; Bullinger's *Decades* of 1549-1551; and his *Summa der Christenlicher Religion*, first published in 1556. These sources provide the most important summaries of Bullinger's doctrine prior to the period during which some have detected a change in his position. While the *Summa* follows chronologically the sources that we will consider in the next chapter—Bullinger's correspondence during the years 1551-1553—it is appropriate that we treat it here, as it purports to be a short summary of the Christian religion and thus complements the more extensive material in the *Decades*.

Accordingly, we will treat these three documents in this chapter, to ascertain the more important features of Bullinger's doctrine of predestination in the first period of his reformatory activity in Zürich.

A. Bullinger's *Oratio* of 1536

Staedtke, in his *Die Theologie des Jungen Bullinger*, claims that, so far as Bullinger's earliest statements on predestination are concerned, they are thoroughly "christological."[4] There is little

---

3. For the purpose of this study, I am dividing Bullinger's theological lifework into two broad phases covering the first and second halves of his term as *Antistes* and successor of Zwingli in Zürich. Fritz Büsser, s. v. "Bullinger, Heinrich," *Theologische Realenzyklopädie,* ed. Gerhard Krause *et al.* (New York: Walter de Gruyter, 1981), 7: 383-84, distinguishes Bullinger's theological development into three phases: an early phase of occasional writings until 1528, a second phase leading up to the publication of his *Decades* in 1549-1551, and a third phase of mature writings whose crowning accomplishment is the Second Helvetic Confession. The two phases I am distinguishing roughly coincide with Büsser's second and third phases.

4. Joachim Staedtke, *Die Theologie des jungen Bullinger, Studien zur Dogmengeschichte und systematischen Theologie,* vol. 16 (Zürich: Zwingli Verlag, 1962): 134: "Bullinger denkt von Anfang an christologisch. Es geht hier auch gar nicht um die schon Augustin beschäftigende Frage, ob die einen selig, die anderen verdammt würden, und darum kommt dem jungen Bullinger auch kaum das in den theologischen Gesichtskreis, was man spätestens seit Isidor

evidence in Bullinger's earliest known comments on predestination of a developed doctrine of double predestination, and where the subject of election is broached, the emphasis rests upon the revealed grace of God in Christ.[5] Election is understood as an implication of the Reformation's concern for salvation *sola gratia*; the believer's salvation is not dependent upon his work or merit, but is wholly dependent upon God's gracious election in Jesus Christ.[6] According to Staedtke, in this earliest period, Bullinger consistently emphasizes the following themes: our election is in, through and on account of Christ; knowledge of salvation is not to be sought outside of Christ and the divine calling;[7] election and faith are correlates, such that the knowledge of election depends upon faith in Christ;[8] and it is therefore impossible to obtain salvation through human merit or the exercise of free will.[9]

More important, however, than the initial and fragmentary references to predestination in Bullinger's earliest writings to which Staedtke appeals, is his *Oratio de moderatione servanda in negotio providentiae, praedestinationis, gratiae et liberi arbitrii,* presented on January 28, 1536.[10] As the title of this lecture indicates, Bullinger treated predestination on this occasion in connection with the related subjects of providence, grace and free will. He did so in the context of contemporary debates regarding the doctrine presented in the writings of Melanchthon, Erasmus,

van Sevilla die gemina praedestinatio nennt." Baker, *Heinrich Bullinger and the Covenant,* 29, on the basis of Staedtke's summary, concludes that "Bullinger developed the themes of his lifelong teaching on predestination in the 1520s. His was a moderate single predestination with a twofold emphasis: God's election to those who believe was in, through, and for Christ; therefore salvation was totally of God's free grace." This conclusion is premature, based as it is upon scattered and occasional references in Bullinger's earliest writings. Greater weight needs to be given to the more comprehensive statements that we are considering in this chapter, together with the kind of evidence adduced from his later writings that we will be considering in subsequent chapters.

    5. Staedtke, *Die Theologie des jungen Bullinger,* 135-36.

    6. *Die Theologie des jungen Bullinger,* 137.

    7. *Die Theologie des jungen Bullinger,* 138. Bullinger, "Kurtze usslegung der epistel zuon *Epheseren* von Paulo" (as quoted by Staedtke: "Der ruoff ist nüt anders, dann eben das zühen Gottes, darmitt er uns zuo Christo zücht, in dem wir erckennend dz heil.").

    8. *Die Theologie des jungen Bullinger,* 138.

    9. *Die Theologie des jungen Bullinger,* 140.

    10. Printed in Johann H. Hottinger, *Historiae Ecclesiasticae Novi Testamenti,* vol. 8 (Zürich, 1667): 763-827. (*HBBibl I,* no. 721) Hereafter *Historiae.* The *Oratio* is treated by Walser, *Die Prädestination bei Heinrich Bullinger,* 163-67, and translated by Schweizer (with some portions omitted), *Die Protestantischen Centraldogmen,* 258-64.

Luther and Zwingli.[11] Though Bullinger only alluded indirectly to these debates throughout the lecture, it constitutes an important statement of his position in the early stages of his work as Zwingli's successor in Zürich.

In the opening section of the lecture, Bullinger defines providence as God's general care for (*cura*) and administration of all things.[12] He then warns against two dangers in the interpretation of God's providence: the Pelagian view which makes God's grace depend upon the exercise of free will, and the Manichaen view which makes God the author of sin and evil. With respect to the second danger, Bullinger insists that God, who is the "Highest" and "Best," always acts according to his own truth and righteousness. Though we are not to measure divine providence according to any human standard, we may be sure that God's ways are beyond reproach. God works in all things, but always in a manner that manifests his wisdom and justice.[13] After briefly defining and summarizing the doctrine of providence, Bullinger concludes his discussion of this subject by emphasizing the *means* God uses in the care, governance and conservation of all things.[14]

11. Walser, *Die Prädestination bei Heinrich Bullinger,* 163-64, notes that Bullinger was likely familiar at this time with the writings and debates of Melanchthon, Luther, Erasmus and Zwingli regarding predestination and free will: "Einleitend weist Bullinger darauf hin, dass gegenwärtig unter allen Fragen keine andere so sehr im Vordergrund der Erörterung stehe. Dies bezieht sich darauf, dass 1521 in erster und 1535 in zweiter Auflage Melanchthons Grundbegriffe der Glaubenslehre erschienen sind, 1524 des Erasmus Angriff auf Luther in der Diatribe de libero arbitrio und Ende 1525 Luthers streng prädestinatianische Antwort De servo arbitrio erfolgt ist. Erasmus antwortet wider Luther 1526 und 1527 mit dem Hyperaspistes in 2 Büchern. 1530 ist Zwinglis Abhandlung über die Vorsehung in Druck gegeben worden, nachdem er im Commentarius vom März 1525 im Abschnitt über den Menschen mit dem scholastisch-humanistischen Menschenbild abgerechnet hatte. Neben Bullinger in Zürich wirkt der von Erasmus beeinflusste Bibliander."

12. *Historiae,* 766: "Ego in praesentiarum usurpabo *Providentiam* pro generali cura & administratione omnium earum rerum, quas suapte virtute condidit Deus."

13. *Historiae,* 769: "Cavendum autem praecipuè *nequid praeter ordinem aequum & justum concipiamus* in administratione providentiave rerum omnium fieri à Deo. Is enim cum sapiens, bonus, aequus & justus fit, omnia opera ejus in sapientia, bonitate & justitia constituta sunt."

14. In the *Oratio* Bullinger follows the traditional order of treating predestination within the context of divine providence and the doctrine of God. This is the order followed by Aquinas, for example, in his *Summa Theologica;* predestination is a *pars providentiae.* However, Bullinger's actual treatment of the doctrine suggests that it belongs as clearly to the *locus* of Christology; he does not treat predestination as simply a subordinate aspect of the doctrine of God.

Of special interest for our purpose is Bullinger's definition of predestination in this *Oratio*. Noting that the terms "predestination" (*praedestinationis*) or "foreordination" (*praefinitionis*) pertain to the salvation and damnation of men, Bullinger defines predestination as God's just determination to grant blessedness to the one who enters into salvation through Christ, and to condemn the other who rejects Christ and the truth, and follows the darkness of the flesh.[15] Though Bullinger links *both* salvation and damnation in his definition of predestination, he immediately guards against the conclusion that these two ends follow from God's will in the same way. On the one hand, he insists that salvation is entirely the fruit of God's free grace, and is not merited by any act of free will. But on the other hand, he warns against an "absolute necessity" (*absolutam necessitatem*) that would make God the author of evil and of every sin.[16] God is in no way responsible for the sin and unbelief of those who perish. Thus, despite the fact that Bullinger's definition of predestination in this *Oratio* includes *both* the election of some and the damnation of others, it is unclear whether it amounts to a doctrine of double predestination.[17] Rather than speaking of predestination and reprobation, Bullinger simply insists that God's will is not the basis for the condemnation of those who reject Christ.[18] In his formal definition, Bullinger speaks of the double outcome of

15. *Historiae*. 777: "Deus enim recta ratione, fine, tramitéque certo alios quidem mortalium beat, eos videlitet, qui per Christum eluctantur ad vitam, alios verò damnat, qui Christo & veritate contemtis tenebras carnis sequuntur."

16. *Historiae*, 777: "Hic verò alij salutem hominis non ad gratiam Dei, sed merito tribuunt libri arbitrij. Alij verò, de electione & fidei dono, sive gratia Dei disserentes, omnia sic rejiciunt in absolutam necessitatem, ut omnis mali, omniúmque scelerum authorem faciant Deum."

17. Cf. Baker, *Heinrich Bullinger and the Covenant*, 31: "Thus Bullinger affirmed a single predestination in 1536. He would not and did not speak of reprobation in terms of predestination because, he felt, to do so would make God the author of sin."

18. Calvin, for example, was prepared to teach quite explicitly that God's will is the ultimate reason for the non-salvation of the reprobate, though he insisted that the actual occasion for the *condemnation* of the reprobate is their own sinfulness. He also taught that God "willed" and did not merely "permit" the fall of Adam. See John Calvin, *The Institutes of the Christian Religion*, ed. John T. McNeill, trans. Ford Lewis Battles, 2 vols. (Philadelphia: Westminster Press, 1960): III.xxiii.1, 3, 8-9. In Bullinger's *Oratio* of 1536, the second of these positions is clearly excluded. Bullinger repudiates any positing of a direct relation between God's will and human sinfulness. Whether he rejects the doctrine of reprobation altogether is not as clear. What he chooses to emphasize is that the reprobate are condemned *because of their willful unbelief and disobedience*. This emphasis, however, is not necessarily incompatible with a doctrine of reprobation, since the condemnation of the reprobate, in Calvin's and in other Reformed theologians' thought, is always *justly on account of their sin*.

predestination; God chooses to save some by his free grace and to damn others. However, he is at pains in his subsequent discussion to clear God of any culpability for the sin and evil that are the occasion for the condemnation of those who do not believe in Christ.

In the remaining sections of the *Oratio*, Bullinger elaborates upon his definition of predestination and warns against several errors that often attend this doctrine. Citing passages from Augustine, St. Paul, and others, he argues that the salvation of the elect is entirely the fruit of God's free and unmerited favor toward his own in Christ.[19] Faith in Christ is a gift of God's grace to his elect; it is not a meritorious work that springs from the exercise of free will.[20] Salvation is not therefore based upon foreseen faith, as though faith were a human work and the ground of salvation. No one may boast before God regarding salvation, for God alone is the author of salvation and the one who gives faith to his people. When it comes to the wicked, however, Bullinger insists that God can in no respect be regarded as responsible for their lost condition. God is neither the author of evil nor the cause of the sin of the non-elect. Though salvation is of God alone, men perish only because of their own guilt.[21] Moreover, the Scriptures clearly teach that God takes no delight in the death of the wicked, but that they should turn from their evil way and live.[22] Those who perish, accordingly, perish because of their own unwillingness to embrace the call of the gospel. Though God gives the wicked over to a reprobate mind, "sin is not of God, but (only) judgment."[23]

In the concluding section of his *Oratio*, Bullinger summarizes his position in terms of the condition of the human will before the fall (*ante lapsum*) and after the fall (*post lapsum*). Though man was able before the fall into sin to live in accord with the will of God, enjoying a true freedom to serve righteousness, the fall into sin has so corrupted and vitiated his nature that the will has become

19. A cursory examination of the citations from Augustine and other church Fathers in this *Oratio* will confirm that Bullinger places himself wholly within the Augustinian exegetical and theological tradition on predestination. However, he repeatedly warns against undue speculation and curiosity in the development of the doctrine.

20. *Historiae*, 781: "Proinde, cum certo constet, fidem esse donum Dei: fidei verò tribui justificationem & salutem: consquens est, salutem, justificationem sive vitam donum esse Dei, quòd respectu gratiae Dei & non operum nostrorum conferatur sanctis."

21. *Historiae*, 784: "Deum, verè optimum maximum, peccati & mortis authorem non esse, sed hominem sua potius culpa perire."

22. *Historiae*, 785.

23. *Historiae*, 796: "Tradidit illos Deus in reprobum sensum. Non ibi peccatum Dei est, *sed judicium.*"

a servant of unrighteousness. "There is always free will in us," Bullinger concludes, "but it is not always good. For either it is free from righteousness when it serves sin, and then it is evil; or it is free from sin when it serves righteousness."[24] The freedom of the will, without the converting and renewing work of God's grace, now consists only in freely sinning, without external compulsion. Unless the will is renewed by God's grace, it has no power to turn to God in repentance and faith.

While this summary of Bullinger's *Oratio* of 1536 offers only a sketch of his earliest comprehensive treatment of the doctrine of predestination, it does provide important evidence of Bullinger's thought at the time it was first delivered, early in the period of his labor as *Antistes* in Zürich. In the title selected for and the development of the argument throughout the *Oratio*, Bullinger clearly wishes to encourage a temperate or moderate handling of this doctrine. Though he is anxious to uphold the Reformation's teaching of salvation by grace alone through the work of Christ alone, he does not wish to do so in a manner that would compromise God's goodness or justice. Salvation is God's gift, freely bestowed upon those whom he has elected in Christ from before the foundation of the world. That some believe in response to the calling of the gospel can only be attributed to the sovereign grace of God in granting faith to them. Bullinger defends sovereign election in this *Oratio*, and condemns every form of synergism which would make salvation dependent upon human effort or will. However, God, who is not willing that any should perish, is not to be blamed for the sin and unbelief of those who are damned. Though all things fall within the scope of God's good providence, we may not conclude that the sin and unbelief of the non-elect is authored in any way by God. All of the culpability belongs to those who refuse the gospel call and will not have faith in Jesus Christ.

B. The *Decades* of 1549-1551

After Bullinger's *Oratio* of 1536 on the doctrine of predestination, the next important source for determining his position is his *Decades* of 1549-1551.[25] The *Decades* are composed

---

24. *Historiae*, 825: "Semper est autem in nobis voluntas libera, sed non semper est bona. Aut enim à justitia libera est, quando servit peccato, & tunc mala est. Aut à peccato libera est, quando servit justitiae."

25. *Sermonum Decades duae, de potissimis verae religionis capitibus. . . .* (Zürich, 1549; *HBBibl I*, no. 179), followed by *Sermonum decas tertia* (*HBBibl I*, no. 180) and *Sermonum decas quarta* (*HBBibl I*, no. 181) in 1550, and the final volume, *Sermonum decas quinta* (*HBBibl I*, no. 182) in 1551. A complete edition, *Sermonum Decades quinqae* was first published in 1552 (*HBBibl I*, no. 184). The *Decades* are available in English translation: Heinrich Bullinger, *The Decades of*

of fifty Latin sermons, probably first addressed to the teachers and pastors of Zürich at their *Prophezei* or gatherings for the purpose of preaching and lecturing on biblical passages and topics. These sermons, gathered together in five books of ten sermons each, represent a full statement of Bullinger's thought at mid-century. According to Edward Dowey, Bullinger's *Decades* are "a major Reformation classic, . . . unchallengeable as his most full bodied and comprehensive theological work, gathering together themes of all his major writings up to that time, and exhibiting the churchly purpose of being a theological source book for pastors to aid them in the preparation of sermons."[26] Both in their comprehensiveness and their influence historically among the Reformed churches, the *Decades* are an unparalleled source for an understanding of Bullinger's theology.

In terms of the structure and arrangement of subjects in the *Decades*, the doctrine of predestination belongs to the third part in which Bullinger treats the doctrines of God and creation. The *Decades* as a whole consist of four major divisions, with a dedicatory epistle:

    I. Ancient Catholic Doctrine (12 documents from the early church)
    II. Soteriology (I.i-IV.ii)
    III. God and Creation (IV.iii-x)
    IV. Church and Sacraments (V.i-x)

Thus, only after an extended defense of the "ancient and orthodox" faith,[27] together with a lengthy treatment of the distinctive

Henrich Bullinger, ed. Thomas Harding, 3 vols., (Parker Society, Cambridge University, 1841-52). The English translations in the following are normally those of the Parker edition; however, in many instances I have modernized the language to conform to contemporary usage. The Latin citations are from the first editions.

26. Dowey, "Heinrich Bullinger as Theologian," 52. Cf. Dowey, "Heinrich Bullinger as Theologian," 56: "I am coming increasingly to the conclusion that the Bullinger of the *Decades* is Bullinger himself—more truly himself than in any other writing." German and Dutch translations of the Decades appeared in 1553 and 1563, respectively, with the title, *Hausbuch*. Dowey, "Heinrich Bullinger as Theologian," 53, notes that in translation these sermons served as a kind of "lay dogmatic for home use" and were widely used by Reformed believers and churches throughout Europe. For an important study of the *Decades*, see Walter Hollweg, *Heinrich Bullingers Hausbuch: Eine Untersuchung über die Anfänge der reformierten Predigtliteratur* (Neukirchen: Neukirchen Verlag der Buchhandlung des Erziehungsvereins, 1956).

27. Bullinger's insistence upon the antiquity of the Christian faith, and upon the catholicity of the Reformation in its defense of "the old faith," is one of the most characteristic features of his thought. Dowey, "Heinrich Bullinger as

teachings of the Reformation (the Word of God as Scripture, faith, justification, love as a fulfilling of the law, the uses of the law, Christian freedom, sin and repentance) does Bullinger take up the subject of predestination in the fourth decade, the fourth sermon.

Just as in the case of his earlier *Oratio* of 1536, Bullinger treats the doctrine of predestination immediately after the doctrine of providence. Within the larger structure of the *Decades*, predestination and providence are both treated under the more comprehensive category of the doctrine of God. Whether or not it was Bullinger's intention, accordingly, to treat predestination at this time as if it were merely a *part* of his doctrine of providence is a difficult question to resolve. Walser, who notes Bullinger's dependence upon the tradition in his location of this doctrine, particularly the precedent of Zwingli, maintains that Bullinger's understanding of predestination is such that it can not be interpreted simply as a *providentia specialis*.[28] Though Bullinger follows the tradition by treating predestination within the doctrine of God, his actual development of the doctrine suggests that it might just as well have been placed within the doctrine of Christ or the application of his saving work. Bullinger's consideration of predestination within the doctrine of God, in other words, may only reflect an unexamined appropriation of the traditional ordering of the doctrinal *loci*.

Bullinger's treatment of predestination in the *Decades* is divided into five sections: first, the definition of predestination; second, the question concerning personal election; third, the problems of doubt and certainty; fourth, the "means" of election; and fifth, the importance of faith and trust. In the following, we will treat each of these in order, and conclude with some related themes that are addressed elsewhere in the *Decades* but not specifically in the sermon on predestination.

After considering providence in the fourth sermon of the fourth decade—a consideration which follows the pattern of his *Oratio* of 1536, emphasizing God's preservation and government of all

---

Theologian," 57, lists it as the first of three "pervasive convictions" in Bullinger's writings. In his treatment of this theme in the *Decades*, Bullinger refers his readers to his *Der Alt Gloub* ("The Old Faith") of 1537 (*HBBibl I*, no. 99) and to his *De testamento* ("Of the Covenant") of 1534 (*HBBibl I*, no. 54).

28. Walser, *Die Prädestination bei Heinrich Bullinger*, 204. Locher, "Grundzüge der Theologie Huldrych Zwinglis im Vergleich mit derjenigen Martin Luthers und Johannes Calvins," *Zwingliana* 8 (1967): 571, says concerning Zwingli's doctrine: "Die Prädestination wird logisch begründet als Spezialfall und Gipfel der Providenz, die aus dem rechten Gottesbegriff folgt, aber ihre Bedeutung reicht weiter: sie ist Fundament der Gewissheit des Heils."

things, and the "means" by which God works[29]—Bullinger turns to the doctrine "of the foreknowledge and predestation of God, which has a certain likeness with his providence."[30] After drawing a clear distinction between God's foreknowledge and pre-destination, Bullinger defines predestination in terms of an eternal decree with a twofold end:

> [T]he predestination of God is the eternal decree *(decretum)* of God, whereby he has ordained either to save or destroy men; a most certain end of life and death being appointed unto them. Whereupon also it is elsewhere called a foreappointment *(praefinitio)*.[31]

This definition is as strong a statement as one will find in Bullinger's writings on the subject of predestination. For in this statement Bullinger explicitly affirms a doctrine of double predestination: the eternal decree of God has a twofold ordination, to save and to destroy; and a twofold end, unto life and unto death.[32]

After setting forth a definition of predestination, Bullinger immediately insists that this predestination is *in Christ*:

> Furthermore, God by his eternal and unchangeable counsel has fore-appointed who are to be saved, and who are to be condemned. Now the end or the decree of life and death is short and manifest to all the godly. The end of predestination, or foreappointment, is Christ, the Son of God the Father. For God has ordained and decreed to save all, how many soever have communion and fellowship with Christ, his only-begotten Son, and to destroy or condemn all, how many soever have no part in the communion or fellowship of Christ, his only Son.[33]

29. *Decades*, IV.iv, fol. 17-20 (PSD 3, 178-84). The emphasis upon the means God uses is evident from Bullinger's definition of providence: "[D]eum omnia sua providentia gubernare, idque pro bona sua voluntate, iudicio iusto, orineque pulcherrimo, per media iustissima equissimaque: quae si quis aspernetur & solum iactitet providentiae vocabulum, fieri non potest ut recte intelligat providentiae negotium" (fol. 18b-19a).

30. *Decades*, IV.iv, fol. 20a (PSD 3, 185).

31. *Decades*, IV.iv, fol. 20a (PSD 3, 185): "Praedestinatio autem decretum dei aeternum est, quo destinavit homines vel servare vel perdere, certissimo vitae & mortis termino praefixo, Unde & praefinitio alicubi eadem appellatur."

32. By distinguishing foreknowledge and predestination, and including reprobation as an element of God's decree, Bullinger seems to repudiate the idea that the non-salvation of the reprobate is simply based upon foreseen unbelief or wickedness.

33. *Decades*, IV.iv, fol. 20 (PSD 3, 186): "Caeterum ab aeterno immutabili consilio prefinivit deus, qui saluari, quive damnari debeant. Finis autem, sive decretum vitae & mortis breve est & omnibus piis perspicuum. Finis

Christ is not simply the means by which God executes his eternal decree, but the *end* of God's predestination. The decree of life and death is to be found wholly in Christ, and is known by us only through him. It is not that we are merely chosen *through* Christ. We are, Bullinger maintains, chosen by God "in Christ, by and through Christ" (*in Christo, per vel propter Christum*).[34] Thus, with respect to the question concerning personal election, Bullinger does not direct his readers to God's decree but to Christ. The question concerning personal election should be formulated in terms of the question of communion or fellowship with Christ. Predestination to life is correlative to fellowship and communion with Christ; predestination to death is correlative to not believing in the name of the only-begotten Son of God.[35] Faith is thus a "most assured sign that you are elected."[36] Thus far and no further, Bullinger adds, will he go with respect to the seat of God's counsel.[37]

Such an answer, however, does not appear sufficient to remove all doubt and uncertainty. Does not our salvation still depend in the final analysis upon "the uncertain election of God" (*incertae Dei electionis*)? To this issue of doubt and uncertainty, Bullinger responds by pointing to Christ as the definitive expression of God's love for his people, as the irrefutable proof that "he is our Father and a lover of men."[38] What greater evidence could there be for God's love than this predestination in Christ, "of the mere grace and mercy of God the Father?"[39] Indeed, we are not to think that God is merciful toward some and just toward others, in the sense that his mercy only summons some to faith and repentance. As the apostle Paul says, "God our Savior wills that all men should be saved, and come unto the knowledge of the truth." According to Bullinger, doubt and uncertainty over God's election ought to be removed by considering Christ: "Truly, in Christ, the only-begotten

praedestinationis vel praefinitionis, Christus est dei patris filius. Decrevit enim deus servare omnes quotquot communionem habent cum Christo unigenito filio suo, perdere autem omnes quotquot à Christi filii sui unici communione alieni sunt."

34. *Decades*, IV.iv, fol. 20b (PSD 3, 186).

35. *Decades*, IV.iv, fol. 20b (PSD 3, 187): "Si communionem cum Christo habes, praedestinatus es ad vitam, & es de numero electorum: si vero alienus es à Christo, utcunque videaris pollere virtutibus, praesdestinatus es ad mortem, ac praeicitus, ut aiunt, ad damnationem."

36. *Decades*, IV.iv, fol. 20b (PSD 3, 187): "Fides ergo certissimum signum est quod electus sis."

37. *Decades*, IV.iv, fol. 20b (PSD 3, 187): "Altius & penitius in conselium divini consilii subrepere nolo."

38. *Decades*, IV.iv, fol. 21a (PSD 3, 188): "Qui pater est, & hominum amator."

39. *Decades*, IV.iv, fol. 21a (PSD 3, 188).

Son of God exhibited unto us, God the Father has declared what great store he sets by us."[40]

After this discussion of doubt and uncertainty, Bullinger takes up the subject of the *means* by which those who are predestined to life are drawn. This drawing takes various forms. Paul was drawn "violently," but this is not the usual manner of God's working. "There are also other ways of drawing, by which God draws man unto him; but he does not draw him like a stock or a block. The apostle says: 'Faith comes by hearing, and hearing by the word of God.'"[41] Furthermore, not only does God use such ordinary means as hearing the word to draw us to himself, but he also "requires our endeavor, which notwithstanding is not without his assistance and grace."[42] That Bullinger does not mean by this a kind of synergism, in which the believer works independently or alongside of God's working, is clear. Yet he also wants to avoid the conclusion that God treats us as "a stock or a block." Paradoxical as it may seem, God demands that we believe, though that believing is not without his assistance and grace.[43] In spite of the weakness of our faith, we ought to seek the Lord's help in strengthening it, that we might trust in him as the one who by his providence cares for us, and in his predestination bestows his grace upon us in Christ.

While this summarizes Bullinger's handling of the doctrine of predestination in the fourth decade, the fourth sermon, it would be incorrect to conclude that this is all that he has to say on the matter in the *Decades*. In an important sense, this sermon presupposes much of the material that precedes it, particularly Bullinger's insistence that salvation is *sola gratia*. In earlier sections of the *Decades*, for example, Bullinger emphasizes that

---

40. *Decades*, IV.iv, fol. 21a (PSD 3, 188): "Certe in Christo filio dei unigenito nobis exhibito, declaravit deus pater quanti nos faciat." Locher, "Grundzüge der Theologie Huldrych Zwinglis," 571-72, indicates that Zwingli held a similar view of the believer's certainty of salvation: "[Predestination] ist Fundament der Gewissheit des Heils. Ihre Formulierung ist eine der originellsten Leistungen Zwinglis: Im ewigen Ratschluss geht die Christusoffenbarung, also die Erwählung Christi, voraus. Auf Grund derselben erwählt Gottes Barmherzigkeit uns Menschen und verbindet uns mit sich, worauf die Gerechtigkeit Gottes uns um Christi willen gerechtspricht und zu Kindern adoptiert."

41. *Decades*, IV.iv, fol. 21b (PSD 3, 190).

42. *Decades*, IV.iv, fol. 22a (PSD 3, 191): "[S]ed quod nostram operam requirit dominus, quae tamen non est extra & sine eius auxilio & gratia."

43. Cf. Bullinger's statement in the *Decades*, I.iv, fol. 16b (PSD 1, 84): "Ubi tamen considerandum venit, Deum in donanda aut infundenda fide non uti absoluta potentia aut miraculo, sed medio & ordine congruo hominibus." As we shall see in Chapter 3, in his correspondence with Traheronus Bullinger is even willing to use the term *cooperatio* in this connection.

faith is wholly God's gift;[44] that our justification is by grace through faith;[45] that Christ is the one Mediator between God and man;[46] that our sinful state is owing to Adam's sin, not God's will;[47] and that the gospel promise is extended to all.[48] Bullinger's doctrine of predestination can not be isolated from these typical Reformation concerns. While we need not give at this time a definitive answer to the question raised above—does predestination properly belong, on Bullinger's view of it, to the doctrines of God and providence?—this summary shows that it certainly belongs as properly to his soteriology and Christology. Predestination expresses the sovereign initiative of God the Father's grace in Christ and his purpose to save his people in him.

There are, however, two aspects of Bullinger's teaching in the *Decades* that remain to be mentioned. These features of his teaching are the so-called "universalistic" passages in the *Decades*, to which the Remonstrants were to appeal during the controversy regarding Arminius' doctrine of predestination,[49] and Bullinger's apparent rejection of a doctrine of the *preservatio sanctorum*. Both of these issues were raised by the Remonstrants, in the context of the debates among the Reformed regarding election prior to and during the Synod of Dort in the early seventeenth century, when they appealed to Bullinger in support of their view. When the Remonstrants made this appeal prior to the Synod of Dort in the Netherlands, 1618-1619, they did so in connection with those passages in the *Decades* where Bullinger seems to teach a universal desire on God's part that all be saved. By means of this appeal to Bullinger's teaching, the Remonstrants sought to avert the charge that they were betraying the Reformed doctrine of election, at least as this doctrine was presented by the Reformers themselves, including Bullinger.

One passage in the *Decades* to which the Remonstrants appealed is found in the first decade, the second sermon: "Our God is the God of all men and nations, who, according to the saying of the apostle, 'would have all men to be saved, and come to the knowledge of the truth.'"[50] As we have seen, this passage of Paul was also cited by Bullinger in the context of his treatment of the doctrine of predestination. But an even more striking

---

44. See *Decades*, I.iv, fol. 16a-17 (PSD 1, 84 *et passim*).
45. See *Decades*, I.vi, fol. 25b-28 (PSD 1, 105ff).
46. See *Decades*, III.x, fol. 118a (PSD 2, 401).
47. See *Decades*, III.x, fol. 107b-108a (PSD 2, 368).
48. See *Decades*, I.ii, fol. 11b-12a (PSD 1, 57).
49. See Hollweg, *Heinrich Bullingers Hausbuch*, 325.
50. *Decades*, I.ii, fol. 11b (PSD 1, 57).

statement to which the Remonstrants appealed is found in decade four, in the first sermon on the gospel:

> And although it may by all this be indifferently well gathered, to whom that salvation belongs, and to whom that grace is rightly preached; yet the matter itself does seem to require in flat words expressly to show, that Christ and the preaching of the gospel belong unto all. For we must not imagine that in heaven there are laid two books, in the one whereof the names of them are written that are to be saved, and so to be saved, as it were of necessity, that, do what they will against the word of Christ, and commit they never so heinous offences, they cannot possibly choose but to be saved; and that in the other are contained the names of those who, do what they can and live they never so holily, yet cannot avoid everlasting damnation. Let us rather hold that the holy gospel of Christ does generally preach to the whole world the grace of God, the remission of sins, and life everlasting.[51]

It is not surprising that these statements by Bullinger, when cited by the Remonstrants, would cause the framers of the Canons of Dort some difficulty when they sought support for their doctrines of limited atonement and unconditional election in the writings of the Reformers.

But it was not only such passages as these that caused some difficulty. There was also the fact that Bullinger in the *Decades* seemed to call into question what the Synod of Dort would later teach regarding the *preservatio sanctorum*. For in his lengthy exposition of the doctrine of true faith, Bullinger expressly states in the *Decades* that "true faith is one alone, which notwithstanding does increase and is augmented, and, again, may decrease and be extinguished."[52] This statement appears to teach

51. *Decades*, IV.i, fol. 139a (PSD 3, 32): "Et quamuis ex his omnibus utcunque colligi possit, quorum sit illa salus, & quibus annuncianda videatur gratia, res tamen ipsa postulat ut expresse & diserte ostendamus, Christum & Christi gratiam evangelio allatam vel annunciatam pertinere ad omnes. Minime enim fingere oportet, duos esse in coelis positos libros, in quorum altero inscripti legantur saluandi, ac necessitate quadam irrefragabili quidem saluandi, utcunque reluctentur verbo Chrsiti & atrocia designent flagitia: in altero autem consignatos contineri damnandos, qui non possint non, quantumius religiose vivant, damnari. Teneamus potius sanctum Christi evangelium generaliter universo mundo praedicare gratiam dei, remissionem peccatorum, & vitam aeternam."

52. *Decades*, I.v, fol. 21b (PSD 1, 101): "Teneamus itaque fidem veram esse unicam quidem, quae tamen augmenta seu incrementum recipiat, denique deficere possit & extingui." Though this remarkable statement seems to deny the idea of a *preservatio sanctorum*, the exposition of true faith that Bullinger provides before and after this remark suggests that true faith is not something that is ever irretrievably lost. See *Decades*, I.iv, fol. 17b-19a (PSD 1, 88-89); I.v,

that even true faith may, under certain circumstances, be extinguished or lost. However, the Canons of Dort, in the fifth head of doctrine, affirm that the faith God grants to the elect will never be utterly or irrevocably extinguished. There is, therefore, at least the appearance of a difference in teaching between Bullinger's doctrine of true faith in his *Decades* and the doctrine that would prevail among the Reformed churches at the time of the Synod of Dort in the early seventeenth century.

We will have occasion in what follows to return to some of these issues. At this point, it is important to note that Bullinger's doctrine of predestination in the *Decades*, while it appears to be quite strong in his formal definition—possibly a doctrine of double predestination—is actually quite moderately stated by contrast to comparable works of Calvin, Luther and Zwingli. In his exposition of the doctrine, Bullinger seeks to guard against any view of predestination that would make God responsible for human sin and evil, or that would not fix the blame for the condemnation of the wicked upon their own unbelief and impenitence. Thus, he emphasizes God's goodwill toward all, a goodwill that is manifested in the person and work of his Son. Because predestination does not exclude but includes the use of the means of grace, no one is absolved of the responsibility to believe and repent at the preaching of the gospel of Christ. Predestination is in, through and on account of Christ. Those who believe, therefore, may know that God has chosen them in Christ. Those who do not believe are justly condemned.

C. The *Summa Christlicher Religion* of 1556

Among those comprehensive works of Bullinger which treat the sum of Christian doctrine, including the doctrine of election, his *Summa Christlicher Religion* of 1556 also merits special attention.[53] Written in German, the *Summa* was first published five years after Bullinger's completion of the *Decades*. By his own testimony, Bullinger prepared the *Summa* to serve as an "epitome" of the teaching of the *Decades*, in response to a number of requests that he provide a statement of his theology that would be more

---

fol. 21b-22b (PSD 1, 101-4). It would be an anachronism to conclude that Bullinger is teaching here the later Remonstrant/Arminian view of the losability of true faith. I will return to this issue in my concluding chapter.

53. *Summa Christenlicher Religion* (Zurych: Christoffel Froschauer, 1556). (*HBBibl I*, no. 283). The *Summa* was translated into Latin (*Compendium christianae religionis*; *HBBibl I*, no. 291) and into French in 1556 (*HBBibl I*, no. 297); into Dutch in 1562 (*HBBibl I*, no. 310); and into English in 1572 (*HBBibl I*, no. 314).

accessible and useful to the general membership of the Reformed churches.[54] Though it was written to be a brief summary of the *Decades*, the *Summa* differs considerably from the former work and so deserves to be considered as a distinct statement of Bullinger's thought.[55]

Indeed, despite Bullinger's own testimony that the *Summa* offers an epitome of his teaching in the *Decades*, there are significant differences in the structure and order of the subjects addressed.[56] The *Summa* is divided into ten articles which treat the following subjects: Scripture (I), God and his works (II), sin and its punishment (III), the law of God (IV, including a consideration of the Decalogue), grace and justification (V), faith and the Word of the Gospel (VI, including a treatment of the Apostle's Creed), prayer (VII, including a treatment of the Lord's Prayer), sacraments (VIII), good works (IX), and death and the end of all things (X). Whereas in the *Decades* Bullinger does not treat the doctrine of God until the fourth decade of sermons, the *Summa* devotes the second article to this doctrine. Of special significance is the fact that Bullinger treats providence in the article on God and his works, but predestination and election are not treated until the fifth article on God's grace in Christ. Thus, in the *Summa* Bullinger separates providence and predestination, a separation which would seem to be in keeping with his own understanding of the latter, although it does not follow the traditional pattern evident in his *Oratio* of 1536 or the *Decades* of 1549-1551.

After considering God's providence in the second article, Bullinger treats, respectively, God's creation of man as good, the fall into sin which is attributed wholly to the creature, and God's merciful and gracious response to this fall into sin by embracing his people within his covenant.[57] Far more than in the case of the

54. Dowey, "Heinrich Bullinger as Theologian," 54, remarks regarding Bullinger's selection of the term *Summa*: "'Summa' (sometimes Summe) is here a German, not a Latin, term, fully naturalized on all levels of German by the year 1500, meaning a brief summation of essential material. So we are not to expect an extended medieval summa theologiae."

55. Though the *Summa* follows the material that will be considered in the following chapter, I am treating it here for two reasons: like his *Oratio* and *Decades*, it offers a comprehensive statement of Bullinger's doctrine of predestination; and it also has a close connection with the *Decades* whose teaching it aims to summarize.

56. Cf. Dowey, op. cit., 55: "[I]t is impossible to reduce in a convincing and coherent manner the structure of the *Decades* to that of its epitome, the *Summa*. The difference, briefly, is not systematic, but schematic and programmatic."

57. *Summa*, II.vii, fol. 31a: "Dises pundts oder Testaments artickel sind/Gott wil unser Gott syn/uns alle gnuege gaeben/ja durch Christum sinen Sun wil er uns vervolkommen und alle himmlische schaetz mitteilen."

Decades, the doctrine of the covenant of grace constitutes a central theme and motif in the *Summa's* presentation of God's saving purposes in history.[58] Within the general setting of the historical administration of the covenant of grace, Bullinger considers the subject of God's grace in Christ, the Mediator, and stresses the great themes of the Reformation: salvation through Christ alone and by faith alone. Our salvation does not come through fulfilling the law of Moses, but through the grace of God in Christ alone, which is "the chief article of the holy evangelical and apostolic doctrine."[59] We are not justified by works of the law but through faith in Jesus Christ.[60] The faith which alone justifies the sinner is, moreover, not a human work but a free gift of God's grace in Christ.[61]

It is at this point, within this soteriological section of the *Summa,* that Bullinger makes his only explicit statement regarding predestination:

> However, God determined in his eternal counsel to exercise his grace through Christ and, at an opportune time that was pleasing to him, to exhibit it to the world. For as God in eternity foresaw the fall of his creature, therefore also he prepared from eternity a remedy, with which he again willed to help the lost world. And he ordained his Son to be sent into the world to assume human nature and to restore fallen man.[62]

58. Cf. Muller, *Christ and the Decree,* 43: "The doctrinal structure which stands out as most original in Bullinger's *Compendium* is the definitive establishment of the gracious covenant of God as the ground for our understanding of Christology and soteriology. Bullinger accords to the covenant a position in relation to his doctrine of God much like the position of an infralapsarian doctrine of predestination."

59. *Summa,* V.i, fol. 57a.

60. *Summa,* V.i, fol. 76a: "Wir wüssend das der mensch durch die werk des gsatztes nit gerecht wirdt, sunder durch den glouben in Jesum Christum."

61. *Summa,* VI.i, fol. 87a: "Diser Gloub ist . . . ein frye gab Gottes / durch den heiligen Geist / welcher durch sin gnad und das wort / des menschen gmut erlüchtet / das es Gott / sin gnad / Christum sin geraechteigkeit und das heil wol und raecht verstadt."

62. *Summa,* V.iii, fol. 76b: "Somlich sin Gnad aber hat Got . . . in sinem ewigen Radtschlag beschlossen / durch Christum Jesum / zuo gelaegner zyt die im gefiel / der waelt zuo leisten. Dann wie Gott von ewigkeit har des menschen faal und verderbung sach also auch er ruft er ouch von ewigkeit har die artzny zuo / damit er der verlornen waelt widerum haelffen wolt / und schluog an das er woelte sinen Sun lassen mensch werden / in die waelt kommen / unnd (sic) den faal widerbringen." Cf. *Compendium,* V.iii, fol. 63b: "Gratiam suam Deus . . . aeterno consilio destinavit in Christo mundo declarare temporibus certis à se constitutis. Nam quemadmodum ab aeterno hominis lapsum praevidit, ita etiam ab aeterno remedia praeparavit quibus mundus perditus reparetur, ac constituit filium suum, qui humanam assumeret

In this reference, Bullinger uses Augustine's common image of Christ as the great physician, and regards election as God's provision for man's salvation, given the fact of the fall into sin.[63] The scope of this election is the "lost world," and thus the definition does not expressly follow the pattern of the *Decades* where those who are predestined to life were placed alongside those who are predestined to death. Rather, God's decree (*radtschlag*) is his provision for salvation through (*durch*) Christ, his calling of a physician able to reverse the effects of the fall within this lost world. Hence, we may say that Christ is our Mediator, "through whom God is gracious toward us and considers us righteous."[64] All of God's promises from the beginning of the world, are fulfilled and expressed in him, for he is our righteousness, sanctification and redemption. Everything that the believer requires for salvation is found in Christ alone. Election in Christ, therefore, constitutes the gracious ground and source for the salvation that is realized throughout the history of the administration of God's gracious covenant.

Though Bullinger's statement of the doctrine of predestination in the *Summa* is less developed than in the case of his *Oratio* and *Decades*, there is no evidence of a substantial difference in viewpoint. Predestination represents God's gracious decision in, through, and on account of Christ, to save his people. The provision of a Mediator for the sins of a lost world, one through whom the gracious promise of the covenant of grace is realized, stems from God's gracious purpose to redeem a people for himself. Though the *Summa* breaks the pattern of treating predestination within the context of the doctrine of God as such and places it in the context of Christology and soteriology, this location is fully consistent with Bullinger's Christological understanding of the doctrine in his earlier works. While Bullinger mentions only God's decision to provide a physician for the sins of the lost world in the *Summa*—there being no explicit reference to a corollary purpose not to save, or decree of reprobation—this is consistent with his exposition of his definition in the *Decades*. This is especially true if

naturam, in mundum mittere, per quem lapsus hominis restituatur ac reparetur."

63. Commenting on this, Muller, *Christ and the Decree*, 42, correctly observes that "The formulation is infralapsarian: God determined from eternity to exercise his grace and to exhibit it to his world through Christ, which is to say that God in eternity foresaw the fall of his creature and therefore also eternally prepared a remedy according to which he ordained his Son to be sent into the world to assume human nature and restore fallen man."

64. *Summa*, fol. 77b: ". . . durch welchen uns Gott gnaedig ist und uns für fromm halt."

we remember the strong emphasis in the latter work upon God's desire to save all.

D. Summary

In his earliest references to predestination, that is, in the *Oratio* of 1536, the *Decades* of 1549-1551 and the *Summa* of 1556, Bullinger's doctrine is characterized by a Christological and soteriological emphasis. Assuming the situation of fallen humanity, predestination and election express God's saving purpose in, through and on account of Christ. While Bullinger uses the terminology of a divine decree in the *Decades* and the *Summa*, this decree is not treated speculatively or abstractly, but in terms of its end in Christ. We are not to trouble ourselves with curious questions concerning God's counsel, for God's intention towards us is exhibited in the giving of his Son. Though Bullinger follows the traditional pattern of considering the doctrine of predestination within the context of the doctrine of God and providence in the *Oratio* and in the *Decades*, his substantive understanding of predestination suggests that it is not understood merely as a part of providence, as a *providentia specialis*. Rather, his understanding of predestination confirms that it is properly related to the doctrines of Christ and of salvation in him, as is explicitly the case in the *Summa*. Within the order of subjects in the system of Christian theology, the doctrine of predestination addresses God's eternal and gracious purpose to save his people in Christ.

Whether or not Bullinger taught a doctrine of double predestination at this time is a difficult question to answer. In his *Oratio* and *Decades*, his definitions of predestination indicate that the decree has a twofold purpose, to save and not to save; and a twofold end, unto life and death. The decree of predestination, moreover, is clearly distinguished from God's foreknowledge; the difference between the elect or non-elect is not based upon foreseen faith, since faith is God's free gift to the elect. All of this points in the direction of a doctrine of double predestination, of election *and* reprobation. However, in his subsequent exposition, Bullinger resists any analysis of the *causal nexus* between God's decree and the non-salvation of those who will not believe. Rather than probing this dimension of the divine counsel, particularly any direct relation of God's will to the non-election of the reprobate, Bullinger chooses to emphasize the revelation of God's mercy and good-will toward all in Christ. No one may conclude, for example, from the decree of God that God neither desires the salvation of all men nor sincerely calls them to faith in Christ through the gospel.

Thus, though Bullinger formally affirms a doctrine of double predestination, his exposition of the doctrine tends to *identify* predestination and election, and excludes any elaboration of the decree of reprobation. Bullinger acknowledges, of course, that some are not elect and therefore are not saved. However, when it comes to the ground and occasion for the damnation of the reprobate, Bullinger maintains that this is entirely due to their failure to believe and heed the gospel message which is preached to all without distinction. On the one hand, faith is God's gift to his elect and a "sign," accordingly, of their election. This faith is the requisite human response to the means God uses in drawing men to himself, the preaching and hearing of the gospel. On the other hand, unbelief is the product of a willful refusal to respond to the summons of the gospel. Such unbelief and impenitence are the occasion for the condemnation of the wicked, not the will of God in reprobation. God is in no respect whatever the author of sin, or of the sinful unbelief and impenitence of those who are not saved.

At this point, it would be premature to draw any settled conclusions regarding Bullinger's doctrine of predestination. Certainly, we have not found sufficient evidence to this point to warrant the conclusion that Bullinger authored another Reformed tradition, distinct from that influenced by Calvin and Geneva. Bullinger, in these earlier writings on the doctrine of predestination, wholeheartedly embraces a number of the key elements of the Augustinian and Reformed tradition. Predestination or election is an unconditional act of God's sovereign grace in Christ; it is not based upon the foreknowledge of faith on the part of the elect. Divine monergism in the initiation and bestowal of salvation are unmistakably affirmed. No fallen sinner is able to do any saving good, being subject to the power and dominion of sin. Only the elect, to whom God graciously grants faith and repentance, are able to respond to the gospel summons.[65] All others, though not under any external constraint

---

65. Just prior to the publication of his *Summa* in 1556, Bullinger wrote a treatise on the grace of God and our justification on account of the work of Christ (*De gratia dei iustificante nos propter Christum* [Zürich, 1554; HBBibl I, no. 276]). In this treatise, he explicitly speaks of God the Father as the "first cause of justification" (*primaria est iustificationis caussa*) whose only basis is the perfect work of Christ the Mediator (fol. 4b). He also insists that regeneration, faith and repentance are the fruits of God's gracious purpose of election, not of human merit or accomplishment: "Non quod fides sit veluti meritum & caussa electionis, quae omnino est gratuita: sed quod fides & ipsa sit dei donum, comprehensa in dispensatione vel ordine salutis, quo deus non alios quam credentes agnoscit pro filijs, eligens nos, non quia credituri eramus, aut quia credimus, sed ut credamus & salui fiamus" (fol. 6a); "Sed modo in verbo suo

or compulsion, are unable to respond appropriately to the gospel's call. The only hesitation Bullinger exhibits in his affirmation of the Augustinian exegetical and theological tradition lies in the elaboration of predestination and reprobation. Anxious to guard against the inference that God is the author of the sin and unbelief of the reprobate, Bullinger eschews any investigation of the connection between the will of God and the non-salvation of the reprobate. Whether this eschewal represents a wholesale repudiation of the doctrine of reprobation is somewhat unclear. Certainly, it represents a repudiation of any *formulation* of reprobation that would inappropriately ascribe the authorship of the unbelief of the reprobate to God.[66]

It should also be noted that in none of these earlier writings does Bullinger systematically develop the connection between his doctrine of the covenant and of predestination. Though the doctrine of the covenant is an important organizing feature of his *Summa*, and though it received substantial elaboration in his *De testamento seu foedere Dei unico et aeterno* of 1534, in the writings we have considered, Bullinger does not explicitly draw any connections between these doctrinal loci. That such a connection exists is apparent, no doubt, from the location of Bullinger's treatment of predestination in his *Decades* and *Summa*. The salvation promised in the covenant of grace could only be realized upon the basis of God's provision of a Mediator and Savior. From eternity God purposed to provide this Mediator as the Savior of his elect people, those to whom he purposed to grant faith and repentance at the preaching of the gospel. The doctrine of

nobis designato: neque omnes salutem recipiunt, nisi qui dei consilio se accommodant, qui electi, inquam, in Christo regenerantur, id est, verbum dei audiunt, credunt, orant, poenitent. Caeterum illa omnia non ex nobis ipsis aut viribus nostris, sed ex deo proficiscuntur, ac gratis, non propter ulla praecedentia & praeparatoria opera a deo conceduntur" (fol. 8a). By means of the administration of the gospel, God the Father's "special grace" toward the elect is manifest, a grace that is not to be confused with the "general grace" of Pelagius or those who teach salvation by human works (fol. 7a). Thus, though Bullinger does not *expressis verbis* connect the doctrines of sovereign election and conditional covenant, the implicit connection between them is clearly set forth in this treatise. Sovereign election undergirds the effective administration of the covenant of grace.

66. This is one of the reasons it is difficult to determine whether Bullinger wholly repudiates the doctrine of reprobation at this point. Advocates of the doctrine of reprobation, including Augustine and Calvin, to mention two outstanding exponents of the doctrine, never taught that God authored the sin or unbelief of the reprobate. Nor did they teach that the condemnation of the wicked is upon the ground of God's will apart from their own culpable sinfulness. Thus, Bullinger's repudiation of the idea that God authors sin or the willful unbelief of the reprobate does not, *by itself*, constitute a rejection of every form of the doctrine of reprobation.

predestination, therefore, constitutes a necessary basis for the realization of God's saving purposes in history through the administration of the covenant of grace. Consistent with Bullinger's stress upon God's use of *means* in the realization of his sovereign and gracious purposes, the covenant of grace is instrumental to the provision of salvation for the elect. What the covenant requires or demands, God graciously grants to his elect. Thus, Bullinger's doctrine of God's monopleuric and unconditional election correlates with his stress upon the covenantal means of salvation, even though he does not explicitly develop this correlation. The conditions of the covenant are only realized upon the basis of God's sovereign and gracious purpose of election.

3

Bullinger's Correspondence on Predestination, 1551-1553

In the previous chapter we considered three important sources for determining Bullinger's doctrine of predestination in the first period of his reformatory labor in Zürich as Zwingli's successor. Each of these sources provides a fairly comprehensive statement of Bullinger's understanding of this doctrine. Though they exhibit a familiarity with the exegetical and theological tradition of Augustinianism, these sources contain very little direct commentary upon or interaction with the views of Bullinger's contemporaries in the Reformed tradition. Undoubtedly, Bullinger wrote as one who was familiar with contemporary debates regarding this doctrine. But in these writings he only alludes to the positions of others, and does not directly comment on the compatibility of his views with theirs. There is little evidence, therefore, that he was self-consciously distinguishing his position from that articulated by other leading figures in the Reformed churches during this period.

However, at the time of the completion of his *Decades* at mid-century, there are two significant, non-systematic sources for ascertaining Bullinger's view of predestination, particularly his attitude toward Calvin's writings on the subject. In the years 1551-1553, Bullinger was obliged to comment directly on Calvin's understanding of predestination on two separate occasions. The first occasion was an important correspondence with Calvin himself, prompted by the case of Hieronymus Bolsec in Geneva. The second occasion was his correspondence with the English theologian Bartholomäus Traheronus, a former student and friend who inquired regarding Bullinger's opinion of Calvin's doctrine of predestination.

Both of these sets of correspondence are particularly significant, as they reveal Bullinger's attitude toward Calvin's doctrine prior to the period during which some interpreters have posited a change in his view toward a more "Calvinistic" position. In both instances, we find Bullinger commenting directly on Calvin's doctrine and presenting a summary of his own view.

Thus, this correspondence is especially important to any evaluation of the distinctiveness of Bullinger's doctrine of predestination within the development of the Reformed tradition.

A. Correspondence with Calvin Concerning Bolsec

Hieronymus Bolsec was an ex-Carmelite monk and physician who had fled France and taken refuge in Geneva in 1551.[1] On October 16, 1551, he publicly attacked, in Geneva, the doctrine of double predestination, arguing that it was not taught in Scripture. He specifically charged the two Reformers, Calvin and Zwingli, with teaching that God was the author of sin. Both Zwingli's *Providentia* and Calvin's writings on the subject of predestination were condemned by Bolsec, for they were full of hard paradoxes that were not warranted by the teaching of Scripture. Bolsec's own position was essentially that of the Catholic church, a position that allowed a cooperation between man and God in the attainment of salvation. Nevertheless, in the course of his attack upon Calvin and Zwingli, Bolsec argued that his doctrine was the same as that of Melanchthon, Brenz and Bullinger.

With this appeal to Bullinger and the other Reformers, Bolsec was responsible for the introduction of Zürich and Bullinger into the controversy. Bolsec himself was immediately imprisoned and tried by the Genevan Senate on the basis of seventeen separate questions. When, in the course of his trial, he made his appeal to Bullinger, the Senate decided to write the ministers of Zürich for their position on the question at issue. This same letter was also sent to the ministers of Basle and Berne on November 14, 1551.[2]

1. See *Registres de la compagnie des pasteurs de Genève au temps de Calvin*, ed. R. M. Kingdon and J. F. Bergier, vol. 1 (Geneva: Droz, 1964), 80-130, for documents and information relating to the Bolsec controversy, including references to Bullinger's works which refute Bolsec (99). For additional information on this correspondence, see Walser, *Die Prädestination bei Heinrich Bullinger*, 168; Fritz Blanke, "Calvins Urteile über Zwingli," *Zwingliana* 11 (1959), 79; and W. Nijenhuis, *Calvinus Oecumenicus* (S'Gravenhage: Martinus Nijhoff, 1959), 101-2.

Philip C. Holtrop, in his *The Bolsec Controversy on Predestination, From 1551 to 1555*, vol. 1, books 1 & 2 (Lewiston: Edwin Mellen Press, 1993), also deals extensively with the Bolsec controversy and its significance for the history of Reformed discussions of the doctrine of predestination. Though an exhaustive treatment of the subject, Holtrop's study is of limited usefulness due to serious flaws in its method and argument. For critical reviews of Holtrop's work, see Richard Muller, *Calvin Theological Journal*, 29/2 (Nov., 1994): 581-89; and Brian G. Armstrong, *The Sixteenth Century Journal*, 25/3 (1994): 747-50.

2. "Lettre des Ministres de Geneve à ceux de Bâle, de Berne et de Zürich," November 14, 1551, in *Ioannis Calvini Opera Quae Supersunt Omnia*, ed. Baum, Cunitz & Reuss *et al.*, vol. 8 (Brunschweig: C.A. Schwetschke, 1863-1900): col. 205-8. Hereafter referred to as CO.

The letter summarized the history of the controversy and indicated that the pastors of Geneva wanted to give all these churches time to respond before the Senate passed judgment. Specific reference was made to Bolsec's repudiation of Zwingli and appeal to Bullinger,[3] and to the fact that Bolsec had unjustly condemned Calvin's *Institutes*.

On November 27, 1551, three responses to the request from Geneva were sent from Zürich: an official letter of the pastors of Zürich,[4] a private letter of Bullinger to Calvin,[5] and a series of *aphorismi* on predestination which Bullinger appended to his personal letter.[6] In the official letter of the Zürich pastors, the suggestion was made that perhaps the Genevan church might have dealt too harshly and precipitously with Bolsec. Moreover, the letter asserted that the views of the Zürich church were already known on this issue, as they were stated in the *Consensus Tigurinus* of 1549. But, in order to give a clear summary of the view of the Zürich church, the letter went on to consider the four points at issue: election, faith, the rejection of those who spurn the gospel, and the order of salvation.[7]

In his personal letter to Calvin, Bullinger also expressed some surprise that Geneva had appealed to Zürich in this case, since the *Consensus Tigurinus* of 1549 contained the view of the Zürich ministry on this question. In any case, Bullinger pointed to his teaching in the *Decades* where he had shown that God is a "lover of man" (*philanthropos*) who, because of his mercy, "wants all men to be saved" (*vult omnes homines salvos facere*).[8] Our justification is of sheer grace, "not on account of works which man has done" (*non per opera quae ipse homo facit*), but for the sake of our Lord Jesus Christ.[9] Moreover, those who are damned are not damned

3. CO 8:207: "Huc quoque accessit quod vestram ecclesiam implicabat. Zuinglium enim prae aliis omnibus damnans. Bullingerum eiusdem secum esse sententiae mentiebatur."

4. *Ministri Turicenses Genevensibus*, CO 8:229-31.

5. *Bullingerus Calvino*, CO 14:207-9.

6. *Aphorismi de praedestinatione*, CO 14:209-11.

7. CO 8:230-31, states concerning election: "Principio constituimus electionem, qua Deus ab aeterno immeritos et peccatores elegit, ac in Christo complectitur, per quem omnia vitae et salutis habemus, omnino esse gratuitam, ac omnem hominis salutem (quod fidei fundamentum est) gratuitae Dei misericordiae esse transscribendam, iuxta illud apostoli: Non est volentis neque currentis, sed miserentis Dei." Faith is further defined as God's gift which is given wholly apart from any human merit or work. Those who are reprobate (*reprobi*) are not defined in terms of a decree of reprobation but as those who do not believe the word of God (*verbo Dei non credunt*) and impiously live in opposition to God.

8. CO 14:208.

9. CO 14:208.

by virtue of a fatal necessity that proceeds from God's will but because they willingly reject the grace of God:

> Therefore, however many men are preserved, they are preserved by the mere grace of God the savior; those who perish do not perish by virtue of being compelled by a fatal necessity, but because they willingly reject the grace of God. Indeed, there is no sin in God; both this and the blame for damnation inheres in us.[10]

Bullinger's letter was not, therefore, a direct answer to the Genevan church's request, so much as it was an indirect criticism of Calvin's doctrine of double predestination as he understood it. The extent to which this was true was demonstrated by Bullinger's hope that the controversy might be resolved amicably and without Bolsec's condemnation. As long as Bolsec attributed our salvation to God's grace alone, Bullinger wrote, the Genevan church ought to seek reconciliation with him in the interest of restoring peace to the church.[11]

To this letter Bullinger appended a series of *aphorismi de praedestinatione*, in which he cited fourteen passages on salvation and damnation from the *Consensus Tigurinus*. With respect to election, Bullinger wrote:

> God the father who is a friend of all, and who has the same respect toward persons in all things, wills that all men be saved and come to a knowledge of the truth. It is also the eternal counsel of the most high God, to bless, to justify and to sanctify men, by remitting sins in Jesus Christ the only begotten Son and sole mediator, by mere grace, on account of his Son alone, who was made man, suffered and died to expiate the sin of the whole world; through faith in Jesus' name, not by merit or by works which man himself has done. On the other hand, however, [it is his counsel] to damn the unbelieving because of their own sin and guilt, because they have not received the savior exhibited to them.[12]

---

10. CO 14:208: "Quotquot ergo homines servantur mera Dei servatoris gratia servantur: qui pereunt, non fatali necessitate adacti pereunt, sed quod volentes gratiam Dei respuerent. Neque enim peccatum in Deo ullum: in nobis id et culpa damnationis nostrae inhaeret."

11. CO 14:208: "Si *Hieronymus* omnia salutis merae tribueret gratiae Domini, nihil nostris viribus, tantummodo ad acutam illam subtilemque quaestionem de reprobatione haereret aut obstupesceret, adde et aequius iudicaret de illis quoque qui et ipsi omnia ascribunt divinae gratiae, nihil nostris meritis, mihi quidem, si ullo modo fieri posset, vestra videretur modestia attrahendus et servandus ab interitu."

12. CO 14:210. "Deus pater omnium philanthropos, et idem in omnes citra personae respectum, vult omnes homines salvos fieri et ad cognitionem veritatis pervenire. Estque consilium Dei Opt. Max. aeternum, beare, iustificare et

In this passage, Bullinger again referred to God's desire that all men might be saved and come to a knowledge of the truth, a passage which, in terms of what we have previously witnessed, runs like a refrain throughout his writings on predestination. Rather than speaking of God's decree of salvation and damnation, he speaks of God's *consilium* to bless, justify and sanctify men in the one mediator, Jesus Christ. This gracious *consilium* is "on account of Jesus Christ, who was made man, suffered and died, in order to provide an expiation for the sin of the whole world" *(totius mundi)*. Those who are damned are damned by virtue of their unbelief, by virtue of their own sin and guilt in rejecting the salvation exhibited to them. In the conclusion of the *aphorismi*, Bullinger repeated the concern of his personal letter that the damnation of those who do not believe must not be understood in terms of a kind of fatal necessity. And he again holds out the hope that Calvin and Bolsec would agree on this question with all "orthodox and catholic" teachers.[13]

A few days later, on December 1, 1551, Bullinger wrote another letter to Calvin concerning the Bolsec controversy. In this letter, he was willing to concede that Bolsec's views might be in error,[14] and assured Calvin that God would guide the Genevan church in this matter. However, Bullinger went on to note that, in the material on the Bolsec case that Geneva had sent to Zürich, there was a reference to a work of Calvin's on the question whether or not God is the author of sin. He indicated that he was interested in this work, for both Calvin and Zwingli (in his *De Providentia)* left the impression that God is the author of sin. For this reason, Bolsec may have been at least partially justified in his charges against them. Bullinger wrote:

> Now believe me, many are offended by your statements on predestination in your *Institutes*, and from that Hieronymus has drawn the same conclusion as he did from Zwingli's book on providence. In fact, it is my opinion that the apostles touched upon this sublime matter only briefly, and not unless compelled to do so and even in such circumstances, they were cautious that

sanctificare homines, condonatis peccatis in solo mediatore Iesu Christo filio unigenito, ex mera gratia, propter ipsum filium, qui homo factus et passus et mortuus expiavit peccatum totius mundi, per fidem in nomen Iesu, non per meritum vel opera quae ipse homo facit: damnare autem incredulos ob ipsorum peccatum et culpam, quia non receperunt servatorem exhibitum."

13. CO 14:211: "Quod si carissimi fratres nostri, M. Joannes *Calvinus* et *Hieronymus* N. et alii, hoc sentiunt, re ipsa conveniunt inter se et nobiscum, qui consensionem hanc retinemus bona fide, et cum aliis orthodoxis atque catholicis. Estque in verbis duntaxat pugna, quam ut ocyssime deponant iubet Christus et sanctorum omnium chorus."

14. CO 14:215.

the pious were not thereby offended, but understood God to desire well for all men, and also to offer salvation in Christ, which itself can be received not by one's own worth but by faith which is truly a gift of God. And indeed the elect are chosen on account of Christ and his grace and not on account of any respect of their own; the reprobate perish truly on account of their own guilt, and not by the malice of God.[15]

In this remarkable statement, Bullinger implicitly criticized Calvin for exceeding the boundaries of this question as they were determined by the example of the apostles. By doing so, Calvin risked giving offense to the pious, since he gave the impression that God does not intend well for all men. For Bullinger, those who are reprobate (*reprobi*) perish by virtue of their own guilt, not because of any malice on God's part (*non Dei malignitate*).[16]

Bullinger's correspondence with Calvin in the Bolsec case concluded with a letter from Calvin to Bullinger in January, 1552,[17] and a response by Bullinger on February 20, 1552.[18] Calvin's letter was written after the Bolsec case was adjudicated and Bolsec had been banished from Geneva. In this letter, Calvin urged Bullinger to keep their disagreement to himself in the interest of unity in the church. Calvin assured Bullinger that the charge that he had made God the author of sin and a tyrant was wholly unjustified. His only concern was to maintain God's grace against Bolsec's teaching that our salvation depends upon our will, a teaching which denied free grace. As to Bullinger's comparison of his view with Zwingli's, this was unfair, for Zwingli's "hard paradoxes" did not properly represent Calvin's own position.[19] Upon receiving this letter, Bullinger heeded Calvin's request and did not mention it to any of his colleagues. In his own

15. CO 14:215. "Nam mihi crede plures offendi tuis Institutionibus de Praedestinatione editis, ac illud colligere quod collegit ex *Zwinglii* libro de providentia *Hieronymus*. Mea quidem sententia paucis sublimen hanc causam attigerunt apostoli, nec nisi coacti, eamque sic moderati sunt ne quid inde offenderentur pii, sed omnes intelligerent Deum bene velle omnibus hominibus, ac in Christo offere salutem, quam ipsi, non sua virtute sed fide, vero Dei dono, recipere possint, adeoque propter Christum et gratiam eius et non ullo sui respectu electi sint, reprobi vero sua culpa non Dei malignitate, perire."

16. It is not surprising that Calvin was disappointed and hurt by this letter of Bullinger. See *Calvinus Farello*, December 8, 1551, CO 14:218, for an expression of this to Farel.

17. *Calvinus Bullingero*, January 1552, CO 14:251-54.

18. *Bullingerus Calvino*, February 20, 1552, CO 14:289-90.

19. CO 14:253: "Obstupui sane quum in tuis literis legerem, docendi genus quo utor multis bonis viris displicere, sicuti et Zwingliano *Hieronymus* offenditur. Obsecro quid simile? *Zwinglii* enim libellus, ut familiariter inter nos loquamur, tam duris paradoxis refertus est, ut longissime ab ea quam adhibui moderatione distet."

response to Calvin, however, he raised the question again whether or not God was the author of evil on Calvin's view:

> That God not only foresaw but also predestined and dispensed the fall of Adam, this seems to be a manner of speaking about the origin of evil and the cause of sin which can be turned around so that God himself is the author. It seems harsh to me, to assert that as many as those whom God has created for mortal destruction, he, in order to attain his goal, has deprived of the facility to hear his word, and indeed blinds by the preaching, and that therefore the universal promises of God . . . pertain, strictly speaking, to only a few.[20]

With this statement, Bullinger gave expression to his concern that Calvin's position tended to make God the author of sin, since God was said not only to foresee (*praevidisse*) but also to predestine (*praedestinasse*) and to administer (*dispensasse*) Adam's fall. Moreover, he took issue with the doctrine, which was Augustine's as well, that the universal promises of the gospel pertain to only a few, and that the hearing and preaching of the gospel serve only to harden the hearts of those whom God has created for death.[21]

B. Correspondence with Bartholomäus Traheronus, 1553

It is not surprising that news of Bullinger's disagreement with Calvin would be reported elsewhere among the Reformed churches. That this occurred is substantiated by a letter from Traheronus, an English theologian, to Bullinger on September 10, 1552.[22] Traheronus had spent some time in Zürich in 1536-1537, at which time he had been befriended by Bullinger. Thus he wrote as one who was an acquaintance of Bullinger and aware of his thought on the doctrine of predestination.[23]

20. CO 14:289-90: "Deum non tantum praevidisse sed praedestinasse et dispensasse lapsum Adami, huiusmodi esse videtur ex quo origo mali causaque peccati in ipsum possit reflecti Deum autorem. Durum mihi esse videtur, asserere Deum eos quos in mortis creavit exitium, ut in finem suum perveniant, audiendi verbi sui facultate privare, adeoque et per praedicationem excaecare, ideoque promissiones Dei universales . . . ad pauculos duntaxat pertinere."

21. In a letter, dated November 2, 1555, CO 15:855, Bullinger expressed the same concern: "Abstinendum itaque puto ab huiusmodi loquutionibus: Adamum ita esse conditum ut non potuerit non peccare: Qui peccant, eos omnino ex destinato Dei consilio peccare . . . . Deum non esse autorem peccati vel malorum; peccata oriri ex homine, nulla necessitate sed voluntate: promissiones salutis esse universales, non ad paucos contrahendas: salvari gratia mera Dei credentes: non credentes sua culpa non credere et damnari."

22. *Trahero Bullingero*, September 10, 1552, CO 14:359-60.

23. Cf. Schweizer, *Die Protestantischen Centraldogmen*, 265; Kolfhaus, "Der Verkehr Calvins mit Bullinger," 81.

In his letter, he reported that in England it was thought that Bullinger had adopted the position of Melanchthon on providence, predestination and free will. Traheronus himself sided with the doctrine of Calvin, and explicitly referred to Calvin's essay on predestination against Pighius.[24] This essay expounded the opinion of Traheronus and his colleagues in England in a most excellent manner. His question, however, for Bullinger was: did Bullinger also teach the same doctrine? What was the opinion in Zürich on providence, predestination, free will and related issues? Traheronus then closed his letter with the hope that Bullinger would prove that he held to the same teaching.[25]

Bullinger's response, the original copy of which is no longer extant, was entitled *de providentia Dei eiusdemque prae-destinatione electione ac reprobatione, deque libero arbitrio et quod Deus non sit autor peccati.*[26] The letter amounted to a substantial treatise in which Bullinger dealt with providence, the threefold status of the human will, and predestination. In the letter, he sought to distance himself from Melanchthon's synergism without embracing the strong statements of Calvin on predestination. His position, he argued, was the same as that which had always been regarded by the church as holy and just.

24. CO 14:359. It is not suprising that Bullinger would be associated with Melanchthon, since he always appreciated his teaching and valued their friendship. Cf. Carl Pestalozzi, *Henrich Bullinger,* 218ff.

25. CO 14:359.

26. In the following I will be using the copy in the CO 14, col. 480-90. Schweizer, *Die Protestantischen Centraldogmen,* 267ff., confuses this letter of March 3, 1553, with three treatises from Peter Martyr Vermigli's *Loci Communes.* Cf. Walser, *Die Prädestination bei Heinrich Bullinger,* 200; Ritschl, *Die reformierte Theologie,* 249. The source of this confusion is the statement in the Genevan edition of Vermigli's *Loci* (1626) where, after the title "loci communes eiusdem authoris, de libero arbitrio, providentia, praedestinatione et de causa peccati," the editor wrote "est Bullinger opus."

The original basis for this editor's confusion lies in Bullinger's *Diarium* (44), where reference is made to a seven-part work with a similar title ("de providentia Dei, Deum non esse authorem mali, de libero arbitrio, de praedestinatione, de electione"), written in June, 1553. Walser suggests quite plausibly that this may have been a reworked version of the letter to Traheronus (194). In any case, the three treatises in Vermigli's *Loci* are not the product of Bullinger's hand, as they differ substantially in content from Bullinger's other works on this subject (cf. Walser, 201ff.). Thus, the work to which Bullinger refers in his *Diarium* is not to be identified with the work cited in the Genevan edition of Vermigli's *Loci,* and is probably no longer extant. As Walser notes, this confusion is compounded by the fact that the editors of *Corpus Reformatorum* (CO 14:480) refer to Schweizer's translation as if it were from the same source as their copy of Bullinger's letter to Traheronus. Cf. John Patrick Donnelly, "Three Disputed Vermigli Tracts," in *Essays Presented to Myron P. Gilmore, History,* vol. 1 (Florence: La Nuova Italia Editrice, 1978), 37-46, who convincingly demonstrates that these tracts were authored by Vermigli.

Bullinger began by defining providence, not in terms of God's decree, but in terms of his *conservatio* and *gubernatio*.[27] This doctrine was a source of comfort for the believer, since in every circumstance the believer had reason to trust that God would seek the best. Nonetheless, this doctrine raised two questions. First, did not God's providence lead to fatalism and even antinomianism? And second, did it not require that God was the author of sin? With respect to the first question, Bullinger answered: "Indeed, God administers all things, but through means, even though he is not bound by them."[28] We should not separate the commands and words of God from the divine providence (*nec separet Dei praecepta ac verba a divina providentia*). With respect to the second question, he argued that God is the "fountain of every good," who neither destined nor impelled anyone to perform that which was evil.[29] In order to explain how God's providence did not make him the author of evil, Bullinger introduced the traditional expedient of a divine *permissio*. This divine *permissio* was inseparable from divine providence, but it was not an *operatio* or "operation" of God. God neither willed nor impelled anyone to sin; he only permitted what he himself abhorred.[30]

Bullinger followed this section on providence with a discussion of the human will in which he utilized Augustine's distinction between the will *ante* and *post lapsum*.[31] The will *ante lapsum* was completely free to fulfill God's commands, but the will *post lapsum* was greatly incapacitated in its ability to do the good. Although the will of the unregenerate was not completely effaced, it was a slave to and sold under sin.[32] This did not mean, according to Bullinger, that we could no longer speak of a "free" will in the post-fall state. The will was not free in so far as it was a slave to sin, but it retained even for the unregenerate a certain freedom. Even though it was sold under sin, "man is not compelled but commits sin of his own accord and nature."[33] But it was with the regenerate that

27. CO 14:481: "Providentia Dei ea est in Deo conservatio gubernatioque qua curam gerit creaturarum suarum omnium, res inquam potenter conservando et sapienter et iuste gubernando."

28. CO 14:481: "Omnia enim agit Deus sed per media, licet his non sit alligatus."

29. CO 14:482: "Deus enim fons est omnis boni et malum non facit, nec in malum destinat vel impellit."

30. CO 14:483: "Permissio non est operatio."

31. CO 14:485.

32. CO 14:485.

33. CO 14:485: "Et omnino rursus est liberi arbitrii. Quod enim malum et peccatum attinet, homo non coactus sed sua sponte et natura peccatum operatur."

we could more properly speak of a free will after the fall. This free will did not belong to the regenerate person by nature but by virtue of God's grace. Through the work of the Spirit, the regenerate person was able freely to do the good.[34]

In the section of the letter devoted to predestination, Bullinger again began, as was the case in his *Decades*, with a strong definition:

> Furthermore, predestination, preordination, or predetermination—that is the ordination of all things to a certain end by God from eternity. However, the Lord has primarily destined every man, and this is his holy and just counsel, his just decree. Now the election of God from eternity is that he truly elects some to life, others to destruction. The cause of election and predestination is nothing other than the good and just will of God, undeserved in the salvation of the elect, yet deserved in the damnation and rejection of the reprobate.[35]

This definition clearly taught a doctrine of double predestination in some sense.[36] God from eternity, Bullinger wrote, "elects some to life, others to death." The cause for this election was God's good and just will, undeserved in the case of the elect, and deserved in the case of the reprobate. Those who were elect were not elect on account of their foreseen faith, as if their election were owing to their own work. For with Augustine, Bullinger noted that our election is not due to the fact that we believe but we are elected in order that we might believe.[37]

Despite the fact that this definition taught a kind of doctrine of double predestination, Bullinger proceeded to interpret it by insisting that *unbelief* is the occasion for the rejection of some. A

---

34. CO 14:487.

35. CO 14:487: "Porro praedestinatio, praeordinatio aut praefinitio illa Dei ordinatio est qua ab aeterno in certum finem omnia, inprimus autem hominem omnium dominum destinavit, idque sancto et iusto suo consilio, iudicio decretove. Iam et electio Dei ab aeterno est qua quidem alios ad vitam elegit, alios ad interitum. Electionis et praedestinationis causa non est alia quam bona et iusta Dei voluntas indebite salvantis electos, debite autem damnantis et reiicientis reprobos."

36. Cf. J. Wayne Baker, *Heinrich Bullinger and the Covenant*, 37: "Although this bare definition might be seen as an affirmation of double predestination, Bullinger clearly did not mean it as such." This observation by Baker seems to go beyond the evidence. It would be more accurate to say that Bullinger speaks of reprobation in addition to election in his definition of predestination, but he is unwilling to link directly God's will with the condemnation of the non-elect. The pattern in this correspondence is exactly the one seen previously in his *Oratio* of 1536 and his *Decades*.

37. CO 14:487: "Etenim Paulus non dicit Deum elegisse nos quod credituri eramus, sed ut crederemus."

reprobos is one who does not believe (*non credentes esse reprobos*), and the fact that not all believe may not be ascribed directly to God's predestination. The culpability for one's rejection does not lie with God "but in man himself when he rejects the grace of God and does not appropriate his heavenly gifts."[38] All those who believe are assuredly God's elect; all those who reject the grace of God are reprobate. Whereas the gift of faith is due to God's mercy alone, the failure to believe remains due to the unbeliever's refusal to accept the promises of the gospel.

If this interpretation of his definition seems inconsistent with its strong terms, the concluding portion of Bullinger's letter to Traheronus was even more striking with its emphasis upon God's universal promises. Bullinger rejected the position of those who spoke of a small number of the elect: "As a matter of fact, we prefer to insist upon these universal promises and to have a good hope for all."[39] This hope was based upon the fact that we were not to inquire curiously into God's secret counsel (*arcano Dei consilio*), but were to heed the revelation of God's grace through Christ and the apostles. This revelation indicated that God was a "lover of man" (*amator hominum*) who desired the salvation of all.[40] For this reason, the gospel must be preached to every creature. Thus, in an obvious reference to Calvin, Bullinger urged Traheronus to avoid a doctrine of predestination which elicited hate and slander against God, or doubt concerning one's salvation. If Calvin only sought to uphold God's grace against those who boasted of their works, no one would oppose him. But to teach that God not only foresaw but also predestined the fall of Adam was to make God the author of sin. When Calvin spoke, moreover, of God raising up vessels of wrath, and of God blinding and hardening the heart of the unbeliever, he spoke in a way that the church fathers never condoned. Such expressions were not required in order to honor God's mercy and grace.[41]

38. CO 14:488: "Dicimus ergo omnes credentes esse electos et omnes credentes fide esse donatos a Deo. Dicimus non credentes esse reprobos, et quoniam non omnes homines credunt non omnes homines esse electos. Quod autem non credunt et intereunt quidam, non in Deum aut praedestinationem eius culpam reiicimus, sed in ipsum hominem gratiam Dei repellentem nec coelestia dona recipientem."

39. CO 14:488: "Quin potuis urgemus universales illas promissiones et omnes iubemus bene sperare."

40. CO 14:489: "[Q]uod videlicet Deus sit amator hominum, quod hominibus bene velit, quod omnes in Christum credentes elegerit ad vitam, adeoque quod omnes homines velit salvos fieri. Unde evangelium praecepit praedicari omni creaturae."

41. CO 14:488.

C. Summary

In his correspondence with Calvin and Traheronus, it seems evident that Bullinger maintained the essential position on predestination that he took in his previous works on the subject, particularly in his *Oratio, Decades* and *Summa*. Within this correspondence, he had occasion to disclose his unhappiness with some of Calvin's statements on the doctrine. For example, he argued against Calvin's inclusion of Adam's fall into sin within the scope of God's decree. Against this position, Bullinger argued that God foresaw but did not administer (*dispensasse*) Adam's fall. If God actually administered the fall, according to Bullinger, then he could be charged with authoring sin.

Bullinger also criticized Calvin's doctrine of double predestination, at least in the form that he understood Calvin to teach it. Just as in the *Decades*, so also in his letter to Traheronus, Bullinger spoke of a double decree of God which implied that God's will is the ultimate reason *both* for the fact that some are saved and others are not. But in a striking parallel to the *Decades*, he refused to develop this inference, and argued that the loss of some is *in no immediate sense* owing to God's will. It is, rather, owing to the reprobates' rejection of the proffered divine grace. Likewise, in his correspondence with Calvin, Bullinger was anxious to repudiate this inference. Faith, as God's gift to the elect, is the "sign" of election. However, unbelief is the *occasion* for the rejection of others. God does not delight in the death of any, for he desires that all might be saved and come to a knowledge of the truth. If we look only to the revelation of God's grace in Christ, the Mediator for the sins of the whole world, we will avoid curious inquiries concerning the divine counsel and focus upon God's love manifest in his Son.

Accordingly, Bullinger maintained in this correspondence that we must emphasize the universal promises of the gospel, proclaim this message to every creature, and avoid such language as tends to distort God's good will toward his creatures. We ought to retain a good hope for all and avoid language, condoned neither by the apostles nor the fathers, which might repulse or engender hatred and slander against God. Calvin, in this regard, ought not to speak of God creating vessels of wrath simply for destruction; nor should he offend by writing that the hearing of the gospel is used by God only to harden the hearts and blind the eyes of those who are not elect. Such language does not reflect the fact that God is a *philanthropos*, that there is no malice in him (*non Dei malignitate*).

There is ample evidence, then, in Bullinger's correspondence regarding Calvin's doctrine of predestination in the years 1551-1553, that he differed with Calvin on at least two matters: the inclusion of Adam's fall into sin within the divine decree, and the elaboration of the doctrine of reprobation in a manner that did not adequately protect God against the charge of being the author of sin. This does not mean that Bullinger's doctrine differed substantially from Calvin's on the important issues of unconditional election or salvation by grace alone through the work of Christ alone. Bullinger continued to uphold the main tenets of historic Augustinianism on the doctrine of predestination.[42] However, he demurred from the severe form in which Calvin cast the doctrine, preferring to emphasize themes that were, in his judgment, in danger of being muted—themes such as God's good will toward all in the preaching of the gospel, the universality of the promises of the gospel, and the culpability of the reprobate for their ultimate condemnation.

42. No more than in his earlier treatments of predestination does Bullinger in this correspondence express any dissatisfaction with the basic tenets of historic Augustinianism. Nor does he address in an explicit manner the connection between his peculiar emphasis upon the covenant of grace and the doctrine of predestination. The connection is, as we expressed it at the conclusion of the previous chapter, indirect and implicit. The "conditions" of the covenant of grace are realized savingly in the case of those whom God unconditionally elects in Christ and to whom he grants the gift of faith and repentance.

4

Bullinger's Participation in Two Conflicts over Predestination, 1560-1561

After Bullinger's correspondence with Calvin and Traheronus regarding the doctrine of predestination in the years 1551-1553, the question of his agreement with the writings of fellow Reformed theologians would surface again. However, now the question would arise, not in correspondence with theologians at a distance from Zürich, but within the setting of discussions and disputes occurring closer to home in Zürich itself, the seat of Bullinger's influence as Zwingli's successor. Once more, the subject of Bullinger's concurrence with the generally acknowledged position of the Reformed churches and some of their leading theologians would arise. Moreover, even more than in the case of his correspondence with Calvin, these disputes would be intertwined with ecclesiastical politics and developments in the period of the Reformation's establishment in Switzerland and elsewhere.

The importance of these conflicts for our study cannot be too greatly emphasized. According to some interpreters of Bullinger's doctrine of predestination, he shifted during this period of controversy to a more rigorous viewpoint, which was closer to that of Calvin than the viewpoint represented by his previous writings. As noted in our introduction, Schweizer and others, who maintain that Bullinger's doctrine of predestination was finally in full agreement with Calvin's, discern a shift in Bullinger's position in the context of these disputes and discussions in Zürich. This shift occurred, in their judgment, in close association with the conflicts over predestination between Vermigli and Bibliander in Zürich in 1560, and between Zanchius and Marbach in Strassburg in 1561. In both conflicts, Vermigli was a crucial figure, as an opponent of Bibliander in the first, and as the writer of the Zürich *Gutachten* in the second.

A. Peter Martyr Vermigli and the Doctrine of Predestination

Vermigli's involvement in these conflicts occurred after his appointment in 1556 to succeed Konrad Pellikan as professor of Old Testament at the Zürich Academy.[1] Prior to his appointment to this position, Vermigli had traveled widely throughout Europe and established himself as a leading theologian of the Reformed faith. Born in Florence, Italy, in 1499, Vermigli was one of a number of influential Italian theologians, including his good friend, Girolamo Zanchius, who joined the circle of Reformed theologians and exercised an important influence upon the early development of the Reformed theological tradition. After his conversion to the Reformed faith through reading the writings of Zwingli, Bucer and Melanchthon, Vermigli was compelled to leave Italy in 1542. Through the assistance of Martin Bucer, he was appointed to teach Hebrew and Old Testament studies in Strassburg. Thereafter, at the invitation of Archbishop Cranmer, he went to England in 1547 and was appointed Regius Professor of Divinity at Oxford. Thus, by the time of his appointment to teach in Zürich in 1556, Vermigli was a theologian of considerable reputation and influence among the Reformed churches throughout Europe.

Vermigli's doctrine of predestination is itself the subject of some dispute. In his older study of the history of doctrine, Schweizer maintained that Vermigli's doctrine was that of Calvin, and that through his presence and influence in Zürich, Bullinger and the leaders of the church in Zürich came to adopt a fully Calvinistic view.[2] Otto Ritschl, though an advocate of the thesis that Bullinger's doctrine was in the final analysis similar to Calvin's, disagreed with Schweizer's interpretation of Vermigli's doctrine, arguing that Vermigli cannot be called an "eigentlichen Calvinisten," since he maintained a moderate doctrine which linked predestination solely with election and not with reprobation.[3] More recent studies of Vermigli's doctrine of

1. The most comprehensive treatment of Vermigli's life and writings remains C. Schmidt's *Peter Martyr Vermigli, Leben und ausgewählte Schriften* (Elberfeld: Verlag von R. L. Friderichs, 1858). For a brief sketch of his life, see David C. Steinmetz, "Peter Martyr Vermigli," in *Reformers in the Wings*, 151-61. For a summary of his correspondence with Bullinger, see Marvin W. Anderson, "Peter Martyr, Reformed Theologian (1542-1562): His Letters to Heinrich Bullinger and John Calvin," *The Sixteenth Century Journal* 4/1 (April 1973): 41-64.

2. Schweizer, *Die Protestantischen Centraldogmen*, 285ff. Schweizer, in fact, entitles his discussion of Vermigli's role, "Peter Martyr gewinnt die Zürcher vollends für Calvins Lehre."

3. Ritschl, *Die reformierte Theologie*, 268ff. One complication, at least in the older interpretation of Bullinger's and Vermigli's doctrines of predestination,

predestination suggest that, though it bore substantial similarity to that of Calvin, it was nonetheless divergent from Calvin's at some important points.[4]

The most important statement of Vermigli's doctrine of predestination is provided in his *Loci communes,* a collection of Vermigli's lectures, treatises and disputations that was posthumously published by Robert Masson in 1576.[5] Masson organized these writings according to the order of Calvin's *Institutes,* though without distorting the basic structure of Vermigli's thought.[6]

In his treatment of the doctrine of predestination, Vermigli followed a far more "scholastic" and rationalistic pattern than the one we have witnessed thus far in Bullinger's writings.[7] He began with an introductory discussion of two matters: the suitability of the doctrine of predestination for preaching and teaching, and the "logician's question" whether or not there is a divine predestination.[8] Only after addressing these matters, and offering a defense against the objection that predestination leads to a doctrine of "fatal necessity" (*necessitatem quidem fatalem*),[9] did Vermigli take up directly the subject of predestination. In doing so, he began with a broad and general statement of predestination, and then spoke of a positive will of God in election and a negative or permissive will of God in reprobation.

---

was the mistaken ascription of three of Vermigli's treatises on predestination and free will to Bullinger. Schweizer and Ritschl, for example, offer their interpretation of Bullinger's doctrine on this assumption, an assumption which, as we noted earlier (see Chapter 3, fn26), has been disproved.

4. For more recent treatments of Vermigli's doctrine of predestination, particularly within the framework of his Aristotelian scholasticism, see John Patrick Donnelly, *Calvinism and Scholasticism in Vermigli's Doctrine of Grace* (Leiden: E. J. Brill, 1976), esp. 3-41, 116-49; Richard Muller, *Christ and the Decree,* 57-75; J. C. McClelland, "The Reformed Doctrine of Predestination According to Peter Martyr," *Scottish Journal of Theology* 8 (1955): 255-71; and Frank A. James III, "Peter Martyr Vermigli: At the Crossroads of Late Medieval Scholasticism, Christian Humanism and Resurgent Augustinianism," in *Protestant Scholasticism: Essays in Reassessment,* ed. Carl R. Trueman and R. Scott Clark (London: Paternoster, 1999), 62-78.

5. *Loci communes D. Petri Martyri Vermigli* (London, 1576; revised 1583). Hereafter referred to as *Loci communes.* References to Vermigli's treatise on predestination in the following are from the revised edition of 1583.

6. Thus Muller, *Christ and the Decree,* 58.

7. Donnelly, *Calvinism and Scholasticism,* 125-29, and James, "Peter Martyr Vermigli," 52-78, document the influence of Aquinas and Scotus among the scholastics, and of the more explicitly developed doctrine in Gregory of Rimini and Martin Bucer among the Reformers, upon Vermigli's thought.

8. *Loci communes,* III.i.1 (443).

9. *Loci communes,* III.i.5 (445).

In his initial definition of predestination, Vermigli maintained that God in his divine counsel (*consilium*) destined or appointed all things to their particular end.[10] Though the divine counsel includes the election of some unto salvation and the reprobation of others, Vermigli proceeded to link divine predestination most especially with election, and formulated the doctrine of reprobation with the use of the scholastic doctrine of God's "permissive" or "passive" will. In his formal definition of predestination, Vermigli emphasized God's counsel to exhibit his love toward his own in Christ:

> I say, therefore, that predestination is the most wise counsel (*propositum*) of God by which he has decreed firmly from before all eternity to call those whom he has loved in Christ to the adoption of sons, to be justified by faith; and subsequently to glorify through good works, those who shall be conformed to the image of the Son of God, that in them the glory and mercy of the Creator might be declared.[11]

By contrast, in his definition of reprobation, Vermigli maintained that, though it had its source in the divine will from eternity, it was a passive act of God in which he withholds his love from the non-elect. He denied, accordingly, a direct or efficient will of God in the instance of reprobation. Those whom God chose not to save are fallen sinners whom he passed by in the divine decree. Thus, Vermigli defined reprobation as God's decree in eternity "not to have mercy on those whom he has not loved."[12]

Though this represents only a sketch of Vermigli's doctrine of predestination, it illustrates some of the differences between Vermigli's doctrine and the one we have found Bullinger to have espoused until this point. Unlike Bullinger, Vermigli cast the doctrine of predestination in a far more scholastic form, exhibiting considerable dependence upon a Thomist construction of the divine counsel with its distinction between God's "efficient" and "permissive" will. Vermigli, in his careful and extended exposition of the divine will, insisted that all things fall within the scope of the divine counsel, whether by way of direct and positive willing or by way of indirect or permissive willing. He was also prepared to

10. *Loci communes*, III.i.5 (448).

11. III.i.11 (449): "Dico igitur praedestinationem esse sapientissiumum propositum Dei, quo ante omnem aeternitatem decrevit constanter, eos, quo dilexit in Christo, vocare ad adoptionem filiorum, ad iustificationem ex fide; & tandem ad gloriam per opera bona, quo conformes fiant imagini filiii dei, utque in illis declaretur gloria & misericordia Creatoris." As translated by James, "Peter Martyr Vermigli," 75.

12. III.i.5 (451).

develop more explicitly the decree of reprobation, linking it with God's passive will and acknowledging that it parallels in some respects God's decree of election. In these emphases, he exhibited a willingness to explore rather explicitly and fully, in the manner of the scholastic tradition, the diverse aspects of the divine counsel. In so doing, he distinguished himself from the more cautious and restrained handling of the doctrine by Bullinger, at least as represented by the sources we have considered to this point.

However, it should also be noted that Vermigli's doctrine approximated Bullinger's in some respects more than that of Calvin. For example, he shared Bullinger's basically infralapsarian presentation of predestination: God's election to save some assumes the fall of all men into sin (*homo creatus et lapsus*). He also, by linking predestination positively with election and only passively with reprobation, shared Bullinger's resistance to positing any direct connection between God's will and the non-salvation of the reprobate. The fact that some are not saved cannot be ascribed to God's efficient will; they are merely left in their fallen condition, a condition for which God bears no ultimate responsibility. God's will in relation to the reprobate is merely passive, not active.[13] Similarly, with Bullinger Vermigli resisted any attempt to draw a positive connection between God's pre-destination and the fall of Adam into sin.

B. The Conflict Between Vermigli and Bibliander, 1560

The claim that Bullinger came to hold the position of Vermigli on the doctrine of predestination is based in part upon the resolution of the conflict between Vermigli and Bibliander in Zürich in 1560. Since this conflict concluded with the retirement of Bibliander from the Zürich Academy, an outcome with which Bullinger concurred, some students of Bullinger's doctrine maintain that this marked a change in his thinking. When Bullinger concurred with the retirement of Bibliander from his teaching position at the Zürich Academy, this coincided with a shift in his view from a more moderate to a more strict Calvinist doctrine. Joachim Staedtke, for example, in his analysis of the Zürich conflict of 1560, contends that it signaled a change in the

---

13. Cf. Muller, *Christ and the Decree*, 66: "Reprobation remains a negative will, a decision to withhold mediation and to leave some men to a fate of their own making. Clearly, the scholastic foundation of Vermigli's argument is not the cause of a more rigid formulation of predestination but of a less overtly deterministic conception of the decrees." Muller correctly makes this point against the claim of Donnelly ("Calvinist Thomism," *Viator* 7 [1976]: 445, 448) that Vermigli's doctrine of predestination was more strict than that of Calvin.

Zürich doctrine of predestination, including that of Bullinger.[14] According to Staedtke, Bibliander's retirement from the Zürich Academy on February 8, 1560, provides telling evidence that the Reformed church in Zürich had embraced a "Calvinistic" doctrine of double predestination: "On this day, Zürich had decided for Calvin."[15]

The two antagonists in the conflict of 1560 in Zürich were Vermigli and Theodore Bibliander (d. 1564).[16] Bibliander had joined the faculty of the Zürich Academy in 1531 after Zwingli's death, a position he was to hold until his retirement in 1560. He was therefore a long-time friend and intimate of Bullinger, in comparison to whom Vermigli was a relative newcomer. As professor of Old Testament, he was an expert in linguistics, having been trained under Ceporinus, Pellikan, Oecolampadius and Capito. His scholarship and acquaintance with Bullinger notwithstanding, it was his view of predestination which was destined to cause him difficulty and elicit Vermigli's opposition. For, on the subject of predestination, he seems to have had more in common with Erasmus than with the leading Reformers.[17]

The starting point for Bibliander's doctrine of predestination was the good will of God toward all men. The teaching that God willed or necessitated the sinful deeds of men was, in his judgment, a "false" and "pestilent" doctrine.[18] God rather wills the salvation of all, and is in no wise responsible for the sinful deeds of men.[19] Though God's foreknowledge includes the awareness of man's sin, this foreknowledge must be distinguished from his predestination; God knew beforehand that which he himself did not predestine.[20] According to Bibliander, God's predestination or election was merely his general purpose to grant salvation to those who believe the gospel and to condemn those who remain

---

14. "Der Zürcher Prädestinationsstreit von 1560," 536-46.

15. "Der Zürcher Prädestinationsstreit von 1560," 546.

16. For a brief sketch of the Vermigli-Bibliander conflict, see Donnelly, *Calvinism and Scholasticism*, 182-83.

17. Though Bibliander has left no systematic or comprehensive statement of his view of predestination, he did present his views in summary form in a lengthy letter in 1535 to Myconius of Basel, a friend and former colleague in Zürich. This letter is printed in *Historiae*, 691-704, and is partially translated by Schweizer, *Die protestantischen Centraldogmen*, 278ff. For a brief sketch of Bibliander's doctrine, see Staedtke, "Der Zürcher Prädestinationsstreit von 1560," 539-40.

18. *Historiae*, 694: ". . . falsum, pestilens . . . *quo traditur, Deum impellere (NB.) atque necessitate absoluta cogere hominem ad flagitia.*"

19. *Historiae*, 695: "Deus nolens iniquitatem: Haec est voluntas Dei, sanctificatio vestra: Nolo mortem peccatoris, sed magis ut convertatur & vivat?"

20. *Historiae*, 695: "*Primum separo prascientiam & pradestinationem, quod plurima Deus pravidit, qua, ut fiant, non pradestinavit.*"

unbelieving.[21] Those who believe are predestined to life, and those who do not believe are predestined to death. In neither instance is this predestination personal, for this would absolve man of the responsibility of responding in faith or unbelief. The exercise of that responsibility has not been predetermined. According to Bibliander, this understanding of predestination allowed for the possibility that one could lose faith and repudiate God's election.

It is not surprising, then, that Bibliander's doctrine of predestination would eventually become a subject of controversy among the Reformed churches in Zürich. Already in the period of the controversy in Geneva regarding the teaching of Bolsec, Bibliander's position had come up for discussion. When Bolsec appealed to the position of the Zürich churches in his defense, he likely had Bibliander among others in mind. Consequently, during the Bolsec controversy, Myconius of Basel, a friend of Bibliander's, had corresponded with him to inquire about his teaching on predestination.[22] Calvin also, in the course of his correspondence with Bullinger during the Bolsec controversy, complained regarding Bibliander's hostility toward his doctrine and inquired about a treatise Bibliander was rumored to be writing against him.[23] In his reply to Calvin, Bullinger was obliged to come to the defense of "our teacher, without a doubt a pious and learned man," disavowing any plans on Bibliander's part to write against Calvin's doctrine.[24]

By the year 1560, however, after a period of increasing conflict between Bibliander and Vermigli, particularly on the subject of predestination,[25] Bibliander was forcibly retired from the Zürich Academy. Though his position had long been out of step with the predominant teaching of the Reformed churches, Vermigli's presence at the Zürich Academy, and the need to forge a greater consensus on the doctrine among the leading theologians and pastors, made it impossible for Bibliander and his teaching to be

21. *Historiae,* 697: "*Nunc pradestinationis sententiam certissimam & indubitatam profero juxta os Christi Servatoris, & judicis: Qui credit in Filium, in iudicium non veniet: qui vero non credit, jam condemnatus est.*"

22. Bibliander's response to Myconius' inquiry is printed in *Historiae,* 705-6. Though he defends himself against the charge of being Pelagian, the brief statement of his position makes election or reprobation depend ultimately upon what people do with the grace offered to all in the gospel. For a summary of the content of this letter, see Baker, *Heinrich Bullinger and the Covenant,* 39-40.

23. *Calvinus Bullingero* CO 14:514.

24. *Bullingerus Calvino,* May 22, 1553, CO 14:533.

25. See *Historiae,* 829, which records a letter from Vermigli to Calvin on July 1, 1557. In his letter, Vermigli confirms that he had lectured at the Academy on the doctrine of predestination and that Bibliander had responded by publicly attacking Vermigli's position in his lectures.

tolerated any longer.[26] Curiously, in the tradition of reports regarding Bibliander's retirement, two different accounts or explanations are provided. On the one hand, one group of accounts suggests that Bibliander's retirement took place for reasons of health and infirmity. On the other hand, another group of accounts references his dispute with Vermigli, suggesting that his retirement took place for reasons of doctrinal heterodoxy.[27] Since there is no evidence that Bibliander was too old or sick to continue teaching at the Academy at the time, the likeliest explanation of his retirement was his denial of the prevailing doctrine of predestination among the Reformed churches in Switzerland. Of special importance is Bullinger's own report of the incident in his *Diarium* which speaks of a conflict between Vermigli and Bibliander.[28] Thus, it seems apparent that Bibliander was removed from his teaching post in 1560 because his views on the doctrine of predestination could no longer be tolerated in Zürich, and because the position of Vermigli was more in keeping with the position of Bullinger and the leaders of the Zürich church.

The full significance of Bullinger's concurrence in the retirement of Bibliander for an interpretation of his doctrine of predestination remains, however, somewhat unclear. Staedtke's claim that this event represented an endorsement of Calvin's doctrine of double predestination on the part of the Zürich church certainly goes beyond what the evidence warrants. No doubt, Bibliander's retirement did represent a repudiation of his

26. Indirect evidence that Vermigli wanted to rid Zürich of the kind of teaching represented by Bibliander is provided by an interesting letter of Zanchius to Calvin, shortly after Vermigli's appointment to teach in Zürich. Speaking of Vermigli's departure from Strassburg to assume his post in Zürich, Zanchi wrote (*Zanchus Calvino* CO 16:246): "I find this one consolation in Peter's departure—I know that he has been called by divine providence to Zürich perhaps for this purpose, that, besides the other opportunities that the church may afford, he may unteach many in that church of the pestilential doctrine (I tell you this heart to heart) of freewill against predestination and God's grace" (as quoted and translated by Tylenda, "Girolamo Zanchi and John Calvin," 111; from CO 16, col. 245-46).

27. See Staedtke, "Der Zürcher Prädestinationsstreit von 1560," for a survey of these two traditions. The first tradition even includes the suggestion that Bibliander was pensioned because he had become mentally unstable. Staedtke persuasively argues that the primary reason for Biblander's retirement was his heterodox doctrine of predestination.

28. *Diarium*, 64: "Anno praeterito et initio huius anni praestantiss. vir d. Theod. Bibliander morosius coepit praelegere et vellicare d. Martyrem. Convenerunt ergo omnes ministri in urbe et negotium retulerunt ad cos. 30. Ianuarii. Cos. refert ad deputatos studiis. Vocatur ergo ad ipsos, donatur rude 8. Feb., stipendio concesso propter merita egregria."

understanding of a general predestination of all who respond to the gospel by faith. This understanding was undoubtedly disagreeable to the Reformed theologians and pastors of Zürich, including Bullinger, however much he may have esteemed Bibliander as a colleague and theologian.[29] But that it meant a wholesale embracing of Calvin's doctrine by Bullinger and the ministers of the Zürich church seems unlikely. At best, this is an unwarranted inference based upon indirect and ambiguous historical evidence. Furthermore, even were it demonstrable that Bullinger and the Zürich ministers had embraced Vermigli's doctrine of predestination over Bibliander's (which it is not), this would still beg the question whether Vermigli and Calvin were fully agreed in their formulations of the doctrine. Here too the evidence does not warrant the conclusion drawn by Staedtke, since there were, as we earlier noted, some significant differences between Vermigli's and Calvin's doctrines of predestination.

It must also be noted that an important factor in the decision of Zürich to retire Bibliander in 1560 was the ecclesiastical situation at the time. Were the Zürich church to have continued to tolerate Bibliander's teaching at the Academy, its reputation for Reformed orthodoxy would have been imperiled. The unity and consensus of the Reformed churches on the basic tenets of the doctrine of predestination was certainly a matter of paramount interest to the Zürich ministers.[30] Their decision to remove Bibliander, therefore, was surely taken, among other reasons, in order to remove any ground of suspicion regarding the position of the Zürich church.

C. The Zürich *Gutachten* on Predestination of 1561

Shortly after the forced retirement of Bibliander in 1560, Bullinger and the leaders of the Zürich church were compelled once again to address the doctrine of predestination. On this occasion, the dispute regarding the doctrine of predestination

29. Cf. Bullinger, *Diarium*, 64, 76.

30. Baker, *Heinrich Bullinger and the Covenant*, 41, maintains that ecclesiastical politics played a decisive role in the retirement of Bibliander: "The verdict was dictated by the growing pressure exerted by the high predestinarians, by ecclesiastical politics, at least for Bullinger." Though ecclesiastical politics likely played a role, Baker's insistence that Bullinger's concurrence tells us little, if anything, about his doctrine at the time seems to overreach the evidence. Bullinger's sympathies surely were with Vermigli's doctrine, not Bibliander's. At least this much seems to follow from his concurrence in Bibliander's retirement, especially when Bullinger's personal fondness for Bibliander is recognized. One complication in Baker's argument is his assumption, based upon the older literature regarding Calvin and Vermigli's doctrine of predestination, that they were in complete agreement. This assumption, however, is incorrect.

originally arose in Strassburg, in the context of a protracted conflict and controversy between Marbach, a vigorous defender of the Lutheran faith, and Girolamo Zanchius, a Reformed theologian and close intimate of Vermigli. Both Marbach and Zanchius were members of the theological faculty of the College of St. Thomas in Strassburg, and had long been entangled in a conflict that reflected the growing divergence between the Lutheran and Reformed positions on a number of theological topics, particularly that of the presence of Christ in the Lord's Supper.

In 1560, the Reformed church in Zürich entered the fray on behalf of Zanchius by drawing up a series of *Gutachten* or "opinions" regarding his doctrine of predestination, one of the issues in dispute between him and Marbach. Unlike the earlier decision to retire Bibliander in 1560, these *Gutachten* expressly state the view of the Zürich church on the doctrine of predestination. Thus, as a public and formal statement of the Zürich ministers, these *Gutachten* have been regarded as of special importance for interpreting Bullinger's sentiments on the doctrine of predestination at the time. Schweizer, for example, claimed that Bullinger's willingness to sign these *Gutachten* coincided with a shift in his doctrine to a Calvinistic viewpoint. Bullinger's support for Zanchius in this dispute was also adduced by the opponents of the Remonstrants at the Synod of Dort in 1618-1619, to answer their appeal to Bullinger as a kind of proto-Arminian in his doctrine of election.[31] Hence, the belief that this event marked a change in Bullinger's view is one which has a significant history antedating the opinion of Schweizer and others by more than two centuries.

Before we consider the opinions of the Zürich church in this case, a brief history of the conflict is in order. The two figures involved were Girolamo Zanchius and Johannes Marbach. Zanchius (b. 1516) was an Italian Reformer who had been won for the Reformation cause by Vermigli while they were both still in Italy. He and Vermigli left Italy in 1550, with Zanchius arriving in Strassburg on March 15, 1553. Johannes Marbach, on the other hand, was a militantly Lutheran theologian, committed to the establishment of the Lutheran church and its confession in Strassburg. He had been a student in Strassburg from 1536-1539

---

31. The role of Bullinger's doctrine of predestination in the context of debates at the Synod of Dort is a fascinating subject. Johann Jacob Breitinger, *Antistes* of the church in Zürich and leader of the Swiss delegation at the Synod, defended Bullinger against the Remonstrants in a speech before the synod. Breitinger adduced in support of Bullinger's orthodoxy, his signing of the Zürich *Gutachten* of 1561 and his personal request that Vermigli prepare them. For a copy of Breitinger's speech, see *Historiae*, 959-76.

and in Wittenberg where he received his degree in theology in 1543. Marbach was primarily responsible for initiating the dispute between himself and Zanchius since, in his attempt to win Strassburg for the Lutheran wing of the Reformation, he attacked Zanchius on the issues of Christ's presence in the Lord's Supper and the doctrine of predestination, specifically Zanchius' doctrine of the *preservatio sanctorum*.[32] In the course of the conflict, Zanchius prepared fourteen theses, several of which set forth his doctrine of predestination. The Zürich *Gutachten* were a series of comments on these theses, written by Vermigli in order to support not only Zanchius but the Reformed cause in Strassburg.

Though there is some debate among students of Zanchius' theology regarding the extent to which he was influenced by Thomas Aquinas and the Medieval scholastic tradition in his formulation of the doctrine of predestination, some features of his doctrine are indisputable and of special significance to a proper appreciation of the Zürich *Gutachten*.[33] Like Vermigli, Zanchius' doctrine of predestination included a clear statement of the double decree of election and reprobation. God's immutable and eternal counsel includes his election to save his people in Christ, and to leave those who are reprobate in their fallen estate. Though Zanchius treated the doctrine of predestination within the *locus Deo*, the doctrine of God, he articulated the doctrine in an infralapsarian manner; God's counsel to save or not to save concerns men who are regarded as fallen in Adam.[34] A special emphasis of Zanchius, and one which would figure prominently in

32. For brief sketches of this conflict and its importance for the cause of the Reformed faith, see Joseph Tylenda, "Girolamo Zanchi and John Calvin: A Study in Discipleship as Seen Through Their Correspondence," *Calvin Theological Journal* 10/2 (November 1975): 121-35; Schweizer, *Die Protestantischen Centraldogmen*, 418ff.

33. For a comprehensive statement of Zanchius' doctrine of predestination, see Otto Gründler, *Die Gotteslehre Girolami Zanchis und ihre Bedeutung für seine Lehre von der Prädestination* (Neukirchen: Neukirchener Verlag Des Erziehungsvereins GmbH, 1965), 108-22; and Muller, *Christ and the Decree*, 110-25.

34. Muller, *Christ and the Decree*, 116, contests Gründler's claim that Zanchius formulated the doctrine of predestination in a supralapsarian manner, appealing to his *De religione Christiana fides*, an extended confession of faith for the German Reformed churches which he wrote late in his life: "Zanchi views man as *creatus et lapsus* under the decree. . . . His personal confession . . . reflects the norms of Reformed theology, and like the definitions found in his larger systematic works, emphasizes God's foreknowing of the fall as voluntarily produced by man within the divine permission; in other words— quite contrary to Gründler's findings—the infralapsarian position." Gründler, *Die Gotteslehre Girolami Zanchis*, 112, incorrectly concludes that, because Zanchi treated the doctrine of predestination in the *locus Deo* prior to the *locus de creatione*, his doctrine is supralapsarian in form.

his dispute with Marbach, was his doctrine of the *preservatio sanctorum*. The elect to whom God grants saving faith will never fall irretrievably into sin and unbelief, for God preserves believers in the faith which he has given to them.

In the course of defending his doctrine of predestination against Marbach, Zanchius appealed to the Reformed churches in Switzerland, including the church in Zürich, for their assistance. His appeal to Zürich was understandable, since his friend and compatriot, Vermigli, was in Zürich and was likely to defend him against Marbach's charges. Along with this appeal, Zanchius sent a copy of his fourteen theses. Upon receiving these theses and the report from Zanchius, Bullinger asked Vermigli to prepare a series of *Gutachten* regarding them on behalf of the Zürich church. These opinions were prepared by Vermigli and then signed on December 29, 1561, by Bullinger, Gualter Wolf, Vermigli, Simler, Lavater, Wolfgang Haller, Wick and Ulrich Zwingli, Jr. The theses which specifically dealt with the doctrine of predestination were the fourth (the number of the elect and reprobate is determined), the fifth (the irrevocability of grace), the sixth (the once-for-all character of election), the thirteenth (the universal promises of the gospel pertain, strictly speaking, to the elect only), and the fourteenth (the passages of Scripture which use "all," like 1 Tim. 2:4, refer to "all the elect").[35]

In his fourth thesis, Zanchius spoke of a "determined number" of the elect and reprobate: "With God there is a definite number of those predestined to eternal life, as well as of the reprobates predestined to destruction."[36] In their consideration of this thesis, the Zürich *Gutachten* follow a pattern used throughout of quoting verbatim the thesis of Zanchius and then appending a statement of their concurring opinion. However, in their statement of concurrence, the Zürich *Gutachten* subtly change the language of the fourth thesis by removing Zanchius' direct linking of predestination with reprobation.[37] The opinions concurred in

35. These theses, with the Zürich *Gutachten*, are printed in *Historiae*, 843-57.

36. *Historiae*, 846: "Certus est apud Deum tum electorum ad vitam, tum reprobatorum adque interitum praedestinatorum numerus."

37. *Historiae*, 846: "Certum esse quendam numerum apud Deum tam Praedestinatorum ad aeternam vitam; quam reproborum, citra controversiam est." Cf. Hollweg, *Heinrich Bullingers Hausbuch*, 313; Baker, *Heinrich Bullinger and the Covenant*, 43; and Walser, *Die Prädestination bei Heinrich Bullinger*, 185-86. Baker and Walser argue that this subtle change may reflect Bullinger's single predestinarianism and his reluctance to link directly God's counsel with reprobation. However, the opinion, even with this slight change in wording, still affirms a kind of "double" predestination, even though it may be more congenial to an infralapsarian formulation of reprobation as a "passive" act of God's will.

speaking of a determined number of the elect and reprobate. But they fell short of speaking of a *praedestinatio ad interitum*, as was the case in Zanchius' original wording. Nonetheless, the opinions affirmed that the number of the elect and reprobate is determined and proceeds from God's immutable and eternal will.

In his fifth thesis, Zanchius had expressed the doctrine of a *gratia inamissibilis*: "Just as those elected to life cannot be lost and thus are necessarily saved, so also those who are not predestined to eternal life cannot be saved and thus are necessarily condemned."[38] While the Zürich *Gutachten* concurred with this thesis, they carefully guarded it against the misunderstanding that the elect and reprobate act under a kind of compulsion in their response to the gospel. According to the Zürich *Gutachten*, while it was true that the elect could not be lost and the reprobate could not be saved, this was not due to a kind of compulsion or absolute necessity (*necessitatem coactionis*). The necessary salvation of the elect and the necessary condemnation of the reprobate must be interpreted in the scholastic sense of *necessary consequence*.[39] The significance of this thesis was that it underscored the certainty of salvation (*salutis certitudinem*).[40]

The sixth thesis of Zanchius was an even more precise statement of his doctrine of the preservation of the saints: "Whoever is once elected can no longer be rejected."[41] In commenting on this thesis, the Zürich *Gutachten* emphasized that this did not mean that membership in the church was identical with belonging to the number of the elect. Zanchius did not mean to deny that some who belong to the church and were judged to be elect were, in point of fact, not included within God's decree, and vice-versa, that some who may be considered to be rejected were in fact chosen of God.[42]

The thirteenth thesis of Zanchius asserted that the universal promises of the gospel, though they are to be preached to all men, pertain in a special way only to the elect. In their concurrence with this thesis, the Zürich *Gutachten* noted that God only grants faith

38. *Historiae*, 847: "Sicut electi ad vitam periri non possunt, ideoque salvantur necessario; ita quoque qui ad vitam aeternam praedestinati non sunt, salvari non possunt, ideoque necessario damnantur."

39. *Historiae*, 849: "Scholastici consequentiae appellare consueverunt." In his letter to Vermigli, inviting him to prepare the *Gutachten*, Bullinger had singled out this thesis as being particularly "hard" (*dura*) and apt to offend rather than edify the faithful (*majori cum offensione, quam aedificatione proponeretur*)." He concurred with it, however, provided it was "correctly understood" (*sano sensu proposita*). *Historiae*, 834.

40. *Historiae*, 849.

41. *Historiae*, 849: "Qui semel electus est, non sit, nec fieri potest reprobus."

42. *Historiae*, 849-50.

to the elect, though he wants the gospel preached to all without exception.[43] Similarly, in their comment on the fourteenth thesis of Zanchius—that it is not a distortion of Scripture to interpret the language of the apostle Paul that "God wants all men to be saved" to mean "all the elect"—the Zürich *Gutachten* acknowledged that this was true and had been the opinion of Augustine. In their conclusion, after having commented upon each of Zanchius' fourteen theses, the *Gutachten* observed that they contained nothing "either heretical or absurd" (*nihil in eis contineri, vel haereticum, vel absurdum*). Indeed, these theses reflected the common doctrine of the ancient fathers; of the Reformers Luther, Capito, Bucer and Brenz; and of many other illustrious teachers of evangelical doctrine.[44]

On the basis of an examination of these *Gutachten*, it seems evident that Zanchius' theses taught a doctrine of predestination that was more rigorous than the one espoused by Bullinger in the writings we have considered. In his *Decades* Bullinger had expressed his misgivings about the idea of a "determined number" of the elect and the reprobate in his statement on the "two books," if this idea were taken in the sense of a necessity of compulsion. He had also, with the exception of his definitions in the *Decades* and the letter to Traheronus, hesitated to link predestination and reprobation, in the sense that those who are rejected are rejected because of God's will. Moreover Zanchius' doctrine of a *gratia inamissibilis* and of a *preservatio sanctorum* went further than Bullinger's statements in these works. In the writings we have considered, Bullinger preferred to emphasize the universal promises of God, and to maintain that we should retain a good hope for all in the preaching of the gospel. He also, at least in one statement in the *Decades*, seemed to allow for the possibility that true faith might be extinguished. Zanchius' language of the reprobate as "vessels of wrath" who cannot be saved was also absent from Bullinger's previous formulations of the doctrine of predestination. Must we, therefore, conclude with Schweizer and others that Bullinger had now changed his position?

Before answering this question, we should note a few factors that must enter into any evaluation of the claim that these *Gutachten* demonstrate a change in Bullinger's doctrine. In the first place, it is important to acknowledge Bullinger's own misgivings about Zanchius' theses, misgivings which apparently led Vermigli, the author of the opinions, to tone down Zanchius'

43. *Historiae,* 855-56.
44. *Historiae,* 857.

position. In his request to Vermigli to write these opinions, Bullinger stated:

> I do not deny that these propositions could have been in some cases put forth more properly. . . . But since they have been proposed, it is certain, in order that evil interpretation might not be added, that they cannot be rejected. . . . The proposition about those to be damned and those to be saved by necessity seems hard, and, if it were proposed so nakedly to the people, it would be proposed to more of them with offense than with edification. ... The remaining theses regarding predestination, the faith and perseverance of the saints are not difficult to affirm, because they are found in Augustine and could be supported with Scripture passages.[45]

Bullinger apparently was not entirely pleased with the formulation of some of Zanchius' theses, insofar as they exceeded the boundaries of Scripture and the position of the Fathers, as represented by Augustine. Undoubtedly, the fact that the Zürich opinions toned down the position of Zanchius was due to these misgivings. This is evident from their explicit association of predestination with election alone, and not with reprobation, as was the case with the original theses.[46] But it is no less true of their attempt to defend Zanchius' fifth and sixth theses from the misunderstanding that they taught a doctrine of necessity or compulsion.

Of further significance is the fact that Vermigli was the author of these opinions, and that Bullinger's request was motivated by a concern for the harm to the cause of the Reformed faith that would result were Zanchius condemned and Marbach vindicated. The tradition of Strassburg, as it was influenced by Bucer and Calvin, was now threatened by a confessional Lutheranism that sought to undermine the Reformed position in this strategic city. The loss of Strassburg to a rigid Lutheranism would be a great loss to the Swiss Reformed church. That this was Bullinger's concern at the time is confirmed by his own words: "For if he [Zanchius] is removed, they will destroy and ruin the school and the church, which have in other respects been weakened

---

45. *Historiae*, 833-35. See Schweizer, *Die Protestantischen Centraldogmen*, 452, for his partial translation. Cf. Baker, *Heinrich Bullinger and the Covenant*, 43.

46. Hollweg, *Heinrich Bullingers Hausbuch*, 314: "Von einer praedestinatio ad interitum aber ist nirgendwo die Rede." Ritschl, *Die reformierte Theologie*, 270, draws the same conclusion.

enough."[47] Prior to Zanchius' departure from Strassburg, Bullinger was to express similar fears in a letter to J. Sturm, Zanchius' sponsor. In this letter he referred to Zanchius' condemnation as the condemnation of the same doctrine that Augustine had taught, an "old and pious dogma of the church."[48] Thus, the dispute over predestination and the perseverance of the saints exceeded the boundaries of a doctrinal dispute between Zanchius and Marbach. It was also, as Hollweg describes it, a "political" issue; and the Zürich opinions were, in this sense, a political as well as a doctrinal statement.[49] Bullinger was as concerned to defend the position of the Reformed church in Strassburg as he was to defend the "Augustinian" doctrine of predestination.

D. Summary

Bullinger's participation in the retirement of Bibliander from the Zürich Academy in 1560 and his concurrence with the Zürich *Gutachten* of 1561 in the Zanchius-Marbach dispute have been cited by Staedtke and Schweizer as decisive evidence of a shift in his doctrine of predestination during this period. By siding with Vermigli in the case of Bibliander's retirement and by supporting Zanchius in his dispute with Marbach regarding predestination, Bullinger made a choice in favor of a more "Calvinistic" doctrine of predestination, one which was more strict than the doctrine he previously espoused. Whereas Bullinger had previously disassociated himself from certain features of Calvin's teaching, including an explicit development of the doctrine of reprobation, now he embraced completely the doctrine of Calvin as it was expressed in the writings of Vermigli and Zanchius.

There are at least two insurmountable problems with this interpretation of Bullinger's involvement in these disputes. First, it is not clear that, even were Bullinger to have embraced Vermigli's doctrine of predestination, he would thereby have fully concurred with Calvin's position. The usual construction that this represented a choice "for" Calvin's doctrine of predestination fails to reckon seriously with the diversity of viewpoint on the doctrine among theologians like Calvin, Vermigli, Zanchius and Bullinger.

47. *Historiae,* 833. See John T. McNeill, *The History and Character of Calvinism* (London: Oxford University Press, 1954), 273, for the political and ecclesiastical importance of this dispute.

48. Schweizer, *Die protestantischen Centraldogmen,* 452, quotes this letter, dated December 30, 1562, as follows: "Es wäre schrecklich, in einer so berühmten Stadt Augustins Lehre verdammt zu sehen. Schützest du den Zanchius, so schützest du ein altes frommes Dogma der Kirche und hast die Autorität der vornehmsten Lehrer unserer Kirche für dich."

49. Hollweg, *Heinrich Bullingers Hausbuch,* 318.

This construction rests upon the unexamined opinion that Calvin's doctrine of predestination was the uniform doctrine of the Reformed churches at the time. Vermigli's doctrine, however, differed from Calvin's at some points, especially in his understanding of the relation between God's will and the fall into sin, as well as the ultimate non-salvation of the reprobate. Therefore, the most the evidence of these disputes could warrant is that Bullinger fully concurred with Vermigli's formulation of the doctrine of predestination, including the teaching of a doctrine of reprobation in terms of God's passive will. *But this would still leave Bullinger disagreeing, as did Vermigli, with Calvin at certain points.* It would not prove that Bullinger's doctrine was now that of Calvin.

The second problem is even more patent. Because neither of these disputes provoked Bullinger at the time to reformulate the doctrine of predestination in his own words, the most that can be drawn from them is that, in the dispute with doctrines that were synergistic and destructive of the monergism of God's saving and electing grace, Bullinger *undoubtedly embraced the principal teaching of historic Augustiniansim:* salvation is based upon God's unconditional election of his own in Christ, not upon human working or merit of any kind. Together with Augustine, Calvin, Luther, Zwingli, Vermigli, Zanchius and the mainstream tradition of reformational theology at the time, Bullinger was as vigorous an advocate of sovereign election as anyone. Though he might have found some of the formulations of his fellow Augustinians too severe or insufficiently cautious, he fully agreed with their fundamental theological convictions regarding the doctrines of sin and grace. Even where he might have differed in his formulation of the doctrine from others in the Reformed tradition, these differences were not as substantial as his disagreement with any doctrine that made the grace of God in Christ rest upon human initiative or effort.

Thus, to proffer a definitive answer on the basis of these two episodes to the question we have posed—was there a shift in Bullinger's position toward a more Calvinistic view during this period?—would be unwarranted and premature. It would be unwarranted for the reasons adduced. But it would also be premature because, in order to arrive at such a conclusion, we must still consider Bullinger's understanding of predestination as it was set forth after this period. Unless it can be shown that Bullinger expressly taught a revised doctrine of predestination from this time forth, the claim that his position changed during the period of these disputes in Zürich is unconvincing.

5

Bullinger's Doctrine of Predestination in the Second Helvetic Confession

It is fitting that we should conclude our consideration of Bullinger's doctrine of predestination, particularly the question whether it represents a substantial alternative to the doctrine of Calvin and the Reformed tradition, with the statement of the doctrine found in the Second Helvetic Confession (*Confessio helvetica posterior*). For the Second Helvetic Confession of 1566 is not only the best source for ascertaining Bullinger's doctrine of predestination after the period in which his view is alleged to have undergone a development, but it also represents the most mature and complete statement of Bullinger's theology after the earlier summaries we have considered thus far. This Confession, which Bullinger probably began to write in 1561,[1] contains a comprehensive summary of Bullinger's understanding of the Reformed faith, including the doctrine of predestination and election, and constitutes perhaps his most important legacy among the Reformed churches of Switzerland and elsewhere.

Recognizing the need for a new, comprehensive confession of faith for the Reformed churches in Switzerland (after the First Helvetic Confession of 1536, to which he had contributed), Bullinger wrote the Second Helvetic Confession, not only as a statement of his personal confession, but also as a summary and defense of the "catholic" faith of the Reformed churches. When Bullinger first wrote this Confession, he had intended that it be affixed to his will as a kind of bequest to the Reformed churches among which he had served as *Antistes*. Little could he have anticipated the extent to which the Confession would be received

---

1. In his *Diarium* Bullinger wrote: "Scribo brevem fidei orthodoxae ex/positionem" (64). Cf. Ernst Koch, "Die Textüberlieferung Der Confessio Helvetica Posterior Und Ihre Vorgeschichte," in *Glauben und Bekennen: Vierhundert Jahre Confessio Helvetica Posterior*, ed. Joachim Staedtke (Zürich: Zwingli Verlag, 1966), 17.

and embraced among the Reformed churches of the continent.[2] Among Bullinger's writings, none is as well known or far-reaching as this Confession in its influence upon the Reformed tradition.

The place and influence of the Second Helvetic Confession as a statement of the corporate faith of the Reformed churches is undeniable. However, the significance of this Confession for Bullinger's personal theological development and position as well cannot be too much emphasized.[3] More perhaps than any of his other writings, this Confession may be regarded as Bullinger's definitive statement of his understanding of the Christian faith. While certainly more than a private Confession, it retains its character as a personal "testimony" and statement of Bullinger's faith, written at a time when he was keenly aware of his own mortality.[4]

In order to summarize the Confession's doctrine of predestination, we shall begin with a consideration of the place of the doctrine of predestination within the structure of the Confession. Only thereafter will we treat directly the statement of

2. Cf. Pestalozzi, *Heinrich Bullinger*, 420. The Second Helvetic Confession, subsequent to its writing, was translated into 15 languages and published in more than 115 editions. It is arguably the most widely disseminated of the Reformed symbols of the sixteenth century.

3. This significance is aptly summarized by Pestalozzi, *Heinrich Bullinger*, 420: "Diese Confession, zu der Bullinger zweimal Angesichts des Todes sich bekannte, erscheint als das reife Ergebnis seines Glaubenslehre, seiner reichen inneren und ausseren Erfahrung, als der Inbegriff seiner theologischen Ueberzeugung wie seiner kirchlichen Grundsätze, als die ächte wahrhafte Entwicklung und Fortbildung seiner früheren Bekenntnisse, zumal der ersten helvetischen Confession." There is some debate whether Bullinger at first only intended this confession as a personal statement of faith, or whether he intended it from the beginning as a public confession for the whole church. For a statement of the first view, see Koch, *Die Theologie der Confessio Helvetica Posterior*, 11ff.; and E. F. K. Müller, *Die Bekenntnisschriften der reformierten Kirche* (Leipzig, 1903), xxxi. For a defense of the second view, see Dowey, "Heinrich Bullinger as Theologian," 56; and idem, "Der Theologische Aufbau Des Zeiten Helvetischen Bekenntnisses," in *Glauben und Bekennen*, ed. J. Staedtke (Zürich: Zwingli Verlag, 1966), 206-7. It seems to me that Dowey is correct in defending the second view. Though a personal statement, Bullinger, even in the choice of language in his title for the confession, clearly regarded it as a "catholic" confession of the faith of the Reformed churches.

4. Cf. his notation in the *Diarium*: "Scripseram illam anno 1564, cum pestis ingrueret, ut ipsam post me relinquerem et senatui donarem testimonium meae fidei et doctrinae meae confess., ac videbatur nunc Palatino mittenda, quod is peteret certam formam doctrinae etc" (83).

the doctrine and its corollaries, as these are expressed in this Confession.[5]

A. The Place of Predestination Within the Confession

The Second Helvetic Confession begins with chapters on Scripture as the source and norm of Christian doctrine (chapter I); the interpretation of Scripture and the important role of the Fathers, councils and traditions of the catholic church (chapter II); and the doctrine of God, his unity and trinity (chapter III). These chapters express Bullinger's adherence to the reformational principle of the supreme authority of Scripture (*sola scriptura*), and his simultaneous insistence upon the catholicity of the Reformed church's confession of Christian teaching. Immediately after these opening chapters, Bullinger devotes two chapters to the subjects of idols and images of God (chapter IV) and of the right worship of God through the Mediator Jesus Christ (chapter V). Only after these foundational and introductory chapters does the Confession take up a series of doctrines, in the context of which some of the distinctive emphases of the Reformation come to clear expression. These doctrines are providence (chapter VI), creation (chapter VII), the fall into sin (chapter VIII), free will and human power (chapter IX), predestination (chapter X), the person and work of Christ (chapter XI), the law of God (chapter XII), the gospel of Jesus Christ (chapter XIII), repentance and conversion (chapter XIV), justification (chapter XV), and faith and good works (chapter XVI). The concluding portion of the Confession consists of a series of chapters on the doctrine of the church (chapters XVII-XXVIII) and two concluding chapters on marriage (chapter XXIX) and the magistracy (chapter XXX). In its structure, the Second Helvetic Confession coincides closely with what would become the normative and traditional ordering of doctrines in the Reformed confessions and theological systems.[6]

5. The Latin text of the Second Helvetic Confession is found in Wilhelm Niesel, *Bekenntnisschriften und Kirchenordnungen der nach Gottes Wort reformierten Kirche* (A. G. Zollikon-Zürich, 1938), 219-75. References to Niesel's text in what follows are by page number and line number (e.g. 65.17 refers to page 65, line 17). The English translations in what follows are taken from *The Book of Confessions*, 2nd ed. (Office of the General Assembly of the United Presbyterian Church in the United States of America, 1966, 1967).

6. Cf. Dowey, "Heinrich Bullinger as Theologian," 56; and Muller, *Christ and the Decree*, 44. A comparison of the structure of the Second Helvetic Confession with, for example, the Belgic Confession and the Westminster Confession of Faith, illustrates that this order is typical of the classic Reformed confessions of the sixteenth and early seventeenth centuries.

So far as the doctrine of predestination is concerned, it is noteworthy that Bullinger treats it in a separate chapter (X), distinct from an earlier chapter on the doctrine of providence (VI), and immediately following chapters on the fall into sin and on free will (VIII-IX). The doctrine of predestination has, accordingly, an infralapsarian cast: God's election is his gracious purpose to save his fallen people in Christ. It is also intimately linked with the Confession's teaching regarding Christ's person and work, which is articulated in the chapter immediately following. Thus, the doctrine of predestination belongs, within the structure of the Second Helvetic Confession, not to theology proper, but to soteriology and Christology.[7] Predestination is Christologically defined as an election *in Christ*, and is not treated within the context of a consideration of the divine *decretum* as part of the doctrine of God.[8] Unlike the traditional order of theological topics followed by Thomas Aquinas and earlier scholasticism, predestination is not treated simply as a *providentia specialis*, but as the foundation for and expression of God's saving grace in Christ.[9]

In his treatment of providence and anthropology in the Second Helvetic Confession, Bullinger follows closely the precedent and pattern of the previous works we have considered. Providence is defined in terms of God's *conservatio* and *gubernatio* of all things.[10] As in his *Oratio, Decades, Summa* and letter to Traheronus, Bullinger contrasts the biblical doctrine of providence with the Epicurean denial of divine providence. The claim that God "is busy with the heavens and neither sees nor cares about us and our affairs" is termed blasphemous.[11] Contrary to this claim and view,

7. Cf. P. Jacobs, "Die Lehre von Der Erwählung In Ihrem Zusammenhang Mit Der Providenzlehre Und Der Anthropologie Im Zweiten Helvetischen Bekenntnis," in *Glauben und Bekennen*, ed. J. Staedtke, 260: "Das Zweite Helvetische Bekenntnis lässt die christologische Heilslehre mit der Prädestinationslehre beginnen. Mehr noch: Die Christologie umfasst zwei Gebiete, Christus als Quelle der Erwählung und Christus in seiner Gottheit und Menschheit." Cf. the opening sentence of chapter XI (*Confessio*, 235.29-31): "Credimus praetera et docemus filium Dei Dominum nostrum Iesum Christum ab aeterno praedestinatum vel praeordinatum esse, a Patre, Salvatorem mundi."

8. Edward A. Dowey, "Der Theologische Aufbau Des Zweiten Helvetischen Bekenntnisses," 218, notes that providence is also not treated in terms of a divine *decretum*.

9. Cf. Jacobs, "Die Lehre von Der Erwählung," 259.

10. *Confessio*, vi, 228.29-31: "Dei huius sapientis aeterni et omnipotentis providentia, credimus cuncta in coelo, et in terra, et in creaturis omnibus conservari aut gubernari."

11. *Confessio*, vi, 228.46-229.1: "Damnamus ergo Epicureos, providentiam Dei abnegantes, omnesque illos, qui blaspheme dicunt, Deum, versari circa cardines coeli, et nos atque nostra nec videre nec curare."

God's providential conservation and governance of all things is a source of great comfort, for it assures us of God's care (*cura*) for his creation. After having defined the providence of God, Bullinger emphasizes the means God uses in carrying out his government of the creation. God's intimate care for and governance of all things does not entail antinomianism or fatalism, for God works through "means," to which "we are to adapt ourselves . . . in so far as they are recommended to us in the Word of God."[12]

The section of the Confession dealing with anthropology, particularly chapters eight and nine on the fall and free will, echo as well themes witnessed in Bullinger's earlier writings. Since these chapters immediately precede the chapter on predestination, it is apparent that Bullinger wishes to treat the latter within the context of man's fall into sin and inability to save himself by the exercise of his own will.[13]

In chapter nine on the freedom of the will and human powers, Bullinger begins with an exposition of the three-fold state of the human will *ante et post lapsum*. Before the fall into sin, man enjoyed the freedom and power to "both continue in goodness and decline to evil."[14] However, after the fall into sin, the will of the unregenerate, though free in the sense that it is not subject to any external compulsion, is unable to do any saving good.[15] Only through the work of regeneration is the renewed will enabled to do good: "In regeneration the understanding is illumined by the Holy Spirit in order that it may understand both the mysteries and the will of God. And the will itself is not only changed by the Spirit, but it is also equipped with faculties so that it wills and is able to do the good of its own accord."[16] As in his correspondence with Traheronus, Bullinger ascribes some role to the will of the

12. *Confessio*, vi, 229.7-9: "Interim vero media per quae operatur divina providentia, non aspernamur ut inutilia, sed his hactenus nos accomodandos esse docemus, quatenus in verbo Dei nobis commendantur."

13. Cf. Muller, *Christ and the Decree*, 44: "Juxtaposition of predestination with sin and the problem of the will represents a powerful affirmation of soteriological monergism: human inability answered directly by the electing will of God."

14. *Confessio*, ix, 232.7-8: ". . . et in bono manere et ad malum potuit."

15. *Confessio*, ix, 232.17-19: "Ergo quoad malum sive peccatum, homo non coactus vel a Deo, vel a diabolo, sed sua sponte, malum facit." *Confessio*, ix, 232.33ff.: "Proinde nullum est ad bonum homini arbitrium liberum, nondum renato, vires nullae ad perficiendum bonum."

16. *Confessio*, ix, 232.47-51: "In regeneratione, intellectus illuminatur per spiritum sanctum, ut et mysteria et voluntatem Dei intelligat. Et voluntas ipsa, non tantum mutatur per spiritum, sed etiam instruitur facultatibus, ut sponte velit et possit bonum."

regenerate in performing the good (*sponte velit et possit bonum*).[17] The regenerate "in choosing and doing good, work not only passively but actively."[18]

Of special importance in the section on anthropology is Bullinger's reference to *curiosae quaestiones* in chapter eight, on man's fall into sin:

> Other questions, such as whether God willed Adam to fall, and similar questions we reckon among curious questions (unless perchance the wickedness of heretics, or of other churlish men compels us also to explain them out of the Word of God, as the godly teachers of the Church have frequently done), knowing that the Lord forbade man to eat of the forbidden fruit and punished his transgression.[19]

This statement implicitly criticizes Calvin's inclusion of the fall within God's decree, and echoes the argument that Bullinger previously set forth in his correspondence with Calvin in the Bolsec case. Ernst Koch, in his study of the text of the Second Helvetic Confession, has shown that this comment was more severe in its original formulation. In his original draft of the Confession, Bullinger spoke in the context of his implied criticism of Calvin's doctrine of those who raise "unchristian questions." The fact that Bullinger, in the final version of the Second Helvetic Confession, modified this original statement, and even excused those who deal with these questions in response to heretics, was due to the persuasion of Beza and Colladon, who visited Bullinger on February 16, 1566, in order to discuss the possibility of Geneva's endorsement of this Confession.[20] Even in its softened form, however, it retains Bullinger's characteristic reserve regarding any formulation of the doctrine of predestination that would compromise God's goodness or threaten to make him the author of sin.

---

17. *Confessio*, ix, 232.50ff.

18. *Confessio*, ix; 233.11-12: ". . . in boni electione et operatione, non tantum agere passive sed active."

19. *Confessio*, viii, 231.40-46: "Reliquas quaestiones: An Deus voluerit labi Adamum, aut impulerit ad lapsum? aut quare lapsum non impediverit? et similes quaestiones deputamus inter curiosas, nisi forte cum haereticorum aut alioqui importunorum hominum improbitas cogit ista etiam ex verbo Dei explicare, sicut fecerunt non raro pii Ecclesiae doctores: scientes Dominum prohibuisse, ne homo ederet de fructu prohibito, et transgressionem punivisse."

20. Ernst Koch, "Die Textüberlieferung Der Confessio Helvetica Posterior," 39-40.

B. The Doctrine of Predestination in the Confession

So far as the place of the doctrine of predestination in the Second Helvetic Confession is concerned, then, there is a considerable correspondence with the approach and emphasis witnessed in Bullinger's earlier treatises. The doctrine of predestination is infralapsarian in formulation, answering to the need of man, conceived of as fallen and sinful (*homo creatus et lapsus*). Within the framework of a confession of man's sinful and needy condition, God's work of redemption finds its source in the sovereign initiative of his electing grace in Christ. Only the monergism of sovereign electing grace can redress the situation of fallen man, whose will, though free from any external compulsion to evil, has no capacity to perform what is good. Only the provision of Christ as Mediator, whose person and work are the exclusive ground of salvation, can accomplish God's sovereign purpose to save his elect. The doctrine of predestination in the Second Helvetic Confession is framed between the two foci of human sinfulness and the divine purposes of grace in Christ.

Bullinger opens chapter ten of the Second Helvetic Confession by defining the doctrine of predestination exclusively in terms of God's positive purpose of election. Whereas in some of his earlier works (his *Oratio*, *Decades* and letter to Traheronus) the doctrine of predestination included, at least formally, the two ends of election and reprobation, the Second Helvetic Confession simply identifies predestination and election: "From eternity God has freely, and of his mere grace, without any respect to men, predestined or elected the saints whom he wills to save in Christ."[21] Elaborating upon this definition of predestination, which includes only God's gracious purpose to save his elect in Christ, Bullinger closely correlates election with Christ. Those whom God predestines are elect, "not directly, but in Christ, and on account of Christ, in order that those who are now engrafted into Christ by faith might also be elected."[22] Were it not for Bullinger's insistence elsewhere that faith is God's gift to his elect, this correlation of the believer's fellowship with Christ and election could almost be interpreted to mean an election *on the ground of faith*, so closely

21. *Confessio*, x, 234.3-5: "Deus ab aeterno praedestinavit vel elegit libere et mera sua gratia, nullo hominum respectu, sanctos, quos vult salvos facere in Christo."
22. *Confessio*, x, 234.11-14: "Ergo non sine medio, licet non propter ullum meritum nostrum, sed in Christo, et propter Christum, nos elegit Deus, ut qui iam sunt in Christo insiti per fidem, illi ipsi etiam sint electi."

does Bullinger join election with the believer's union with Christ.[23] Similarly, in the only explicit mention of reprobation, Bullinger defines the reprobate as those who are "outside of Christ" (*reprobi vero, qui sunt extra Christum*).[24] No explanation of reprobation is offered in terms of God's will or purpose. It is enough to know that those who are rejected are rejected inasmuch as they have no fellowship with Christ.

After defining the doctrine of predestination as God's free election of his people in and on account of Christ, the remainder of chapter ten is preoccupied with pastoral questions that arise in this context. With respect to the question concerning the scope of election, Bullinger repeats his familiar insistence that "we must hope well of all and not rashly judge any man to be a reprobate."[25] Rather than speculating about the relative number of the elect, whether they be few or many, we should encourage every one to "strive to enter by the narrow door" (Luke 13:24). Although Bullinger does not use the expression in the Second Helvetic Confession, his insistence that no one be rashly considered reprobate, and that believers hold out hope for all, reflect his emphasis in other writings upon God as a *philanthropos* who bears malice toward none. And, although he does not explicitly speak of the universal promises of God, he does speak of God's promises "which apply to all the faithful" and which ought to be the occasion for confidence before God.[26]

The closing sections of chapter ten address the critical question of the believer's assurance or knowledge of election. Consistent with the close and intimate conjunction of election with Christ in his opening definition, Bullinger insists in this section that the believer's relationship with Christ is the basis for any assurance of election. We ought not to ask whether we are elect from eternity "outside of Christ" (*extra Christum*).[27] Rather, it is the preaching of the gospel promise in Christ which is to be believed. For "it is to be held as beyond doubt that if you believe and are in Christ, you are

23. Cf. *Confessio,* xvi, 246.13-16: "Haec autem fides, merum est Dei donum, quod solus Deus ex gratia sua, electis suis, secundum mensuram, et quando, cui, et quantum ipse vult, donat, et quidem per spiritum sanctum, mediante praedicatione evangelii, et oratione fideli."

24. *Confessio,* x, 234.14.

25. Confessio, x, 234.24-25: ". . . bene sperandum est tamen de omnibus, neque temere reprobis quisquam est annumerandus."

26. *Confessio,* x, 235.19-20: ". . . promissiones Dei sunt universales fidelibus."

27. *Confessio,* x, 235.1-2: "Improbamus itaque illos, qui extra Christum quaerent, An sint electi?"

elected."[28] For Bullinger, "being-elect" and "being-in-Christ" are correlated, just as "being-rejected" and "being-outside-of-Christ" through unbelief are correlated. Employing imagery used by Calvin to answer the question of the assurance of election, Bullinger asserts: "Let Christ, therefore be the looking glass (*speculum*), in whom we may contemplate our predestination. We shall have a sufficient and clear testimony that we are inscribed in the Book of life if we have fellowship with Christ, and he is ours and we are his in true faith."[29] It is in this sense, our election and fellowship with Christ being joined, that admonitions are not in vain. As Augustine has shown, "both the grace of free election and predestination, and also salutary admonitions and doctrines, are to be preached."[30] Consequently, Bullinger concludes his discussion of predestination and election with St. Paul's admonition to work out our salvation with fear and trembling.

C. Summary

The location of Bullinger's treatment of the doctrine of predestination in the Second Helvetic Confession coincides with his substantive understanding of the doctrine in his previous writings. Though in some of these writings Bullinger simply followed the classic order of considering predestination within the doctrine of God, the interest of the doctrine, in his formulation and confession, is God's sovereign provision of redemption through Christ. From eternity God has purposed to elect his people in Christ, to furnish a Mediator whose person and work are the basis for their redemption. By placing his consideration of predestination after the doctrine of sin and prior to the doctrine of Christ, Bullinger adopts a systematic arrangement that answers properly to the soteriological and Christological assumptions of the doctrine: God's gracious purpose of election in Christ is the only basis for the salvation of fallen sinners who are incapable of any saving good.

28. *Confessio*, x. 235.4: "[P]ro indubitato habendum, si credis ac sis in Christo, electum te esse."

29. *Confessio*, x, 235.14-17: "Christus itaque sit speculum, in quo praedestinationem nostram contemplemur. Satis perspicuum et firmum habebimus testimonium, nos in libro vitae inscriptos esse, si communicaverimus cum Christo, et is in vera fide noster sit, nos eius simus." Cf. Calvin, *Institutes*, III.xxiv.5.

30. *Confessio*, x, 234.48-49. As in his other writings on the subject of predestination, Bullinger's references to Augustine's writings reflect his standing in the Augustinian exegetical and theological tradition.

One of the outstanding features of the doctrine of predestination in the Second Helvetic Confession is the simple identification of predestination and election. Whereas in some of his earlier works Bullinger spoke of the double end of predestination in election and reprobation, his definition in the Confession omits altogether any explicit reference to reprobation. God's work of predestination is his sovereign purpose to elect his people in, through, and on account of Christ. Chapter ten is, accordingly, entitled *De praedestinatione, et electione sanctorum,* and is intimately and expressly linked with chapter eleven on the person of Christ as the only Savior.[31] Within this context of an identification of predestination and election in, through and on account of Christ, Bullinger only speaks indirectly of rejection or reprobation. The Second Helvetic Confession does not say that the reprobate are *extra Christum* because God has predestined them *ab aeterno ad interitum.* Rather, those who are rejected (*reprobi*) are simply defined as those who are *extra Christum.* In the discussion of the assurance of election, Bullinger appeals to Scripture to emphasize that our election is in Christ and is known through a believing acceptance of the gospel promise in Christ. Election does not exclude God's call as it comes through the preaching of the gospel, for it is precisely through the gospel summons that God calls us into fellowship with Christ, the *speculum* of our election.

If the statement of the doctrine of predestination in the Second Helvetic Confession is compared to Bullinger's earlier writings on the subject, a remarkable consistency and similarity of expression and thought are evident. There is nothing in the formulation of the doctrine in this Confession that distinguishes it in any substantial way from Bullinger's previous handling of the doctrine. Though Bullinger demonstrates greater reserve than in some prior instances in his consideration of the subject of reprobation (the definition of predestination speaks only of election, excluding reprobation), his reluctance to draw a direct connection between God's will and the condemnation of those who are outside of Christ certainly follows the pattern of his earlier writings. The pastoral quality of Bullinger's handling of the doctrine is also evident in the way the Confession echoes themes characteristic of his previous treatments of the doctrine: the good hope that we should have for all, not rashly judging anyone a reprobate; the

31. The language at the opening of chapter eleven makes this link explicit: "Credimus praeterea et docemus filium Dei Dominum nostrum Iesum Christum ab aeterno praedestinatum vel praeordinatum esse, a Patre, Salvatorem mundi" (*Confessio*, xi, 235.29-31).

repudiation of the assumption that the number of the elect is only few; the importance of the means God uses in the accomplishment of his saving purposes; and the assurance of election through fellowship with Christ. Though these themes were by no means unique to Bullinger's formulation of the doctrine of predestination among the Reformed theologians of the mid-sixteenth century, including Calvin, the pastoral and homiletical manner in which Bullinger treats the doctrine of predestination in the Confession bears many tell-tale traces of his earlier formulations. Perhaps what is most remarkable about the statement of the doctrine in the Second Helvetic Confession, then, is the extent to which it represents a kind of *confirmation* or *codification* of Bullinger's previous statements.

One interesting feature of the Second Helvetic Confession is the relatively small place that it gives to the doctrine of the covenant. Considering the importance of the doctrine of the covenant in Bullinger's thought and writings, it is striking that the Second Helvetic Confession only mentions the doctrine explicitly in connection with the subject of infant baptism. Though it is possible to argue that elements of the doctrine of the covenant are implicit throughout the Confession, the absence of any substantial or explicit reference to the doctrine throughout certainly raises questions regarding the thesis that Bullinger systematically organized his thought in terms of this doctrine.[32] The reader is left to surmise, as in the case of Bullinger's other treatments of predestination, what is the relation or connection between predestination and covenant. That connection, as we have previously summarized it, is not difficult to discern. Those whom God the Father has elected to save in Christ, whose salvation was the occasion for the predestination of the Son from eternity to be the Savior of the world, are saved through the administration of

---

32. Cf. Koch, *Die Theologie der Confessio Helvetica Posterior,* 425-30, and Baker, *Heinrich Bullinger and the Covenant,* 47-54, who argue that the doctrine of the covenant is the systematic and organizing principle of Bullinger's thought in the Second Helvetic Confession, even though it is more implicit than explicit. Dowey, "Heinrich Bullinger as Theologian: Thematic, Comprehensive, Schematic," 43-50, properly demurs, however, arguing that the doctrine of the covenant is one of several "pervasive convictions" in Bullinger's writings, but not "a single 'principal formative and organizing factor'": "Again, our solution should not be to smuggle the covenant into the Second Helvetic Confession. Our very real problem is to find out what it means that after about forty years of reflection, of preaching, of teaching, and of writing—which included about a dozen full, formal, comprehensive presentations of his theological thought— Bullinger's masterpiece, the *Confessio Helvetica Posterior,* does not contain a doctrine that he from time to time elsewhere called the *scopus Scripturae,* and *scopus legis, prophetarum, et apostolorum*" (45).

the covenant of grace of which Christ is the Mediator. The covenant of grace, administered through the preaching of the gospel and the holy sacraments, is the instrument through which God grants faith to the elect and secures their salvation through fellowship with Christ. Though Bullinger does not explicitly or systematically draw these and other lines of connection between the doctrines of predestination and covenant, they lie close to the surface of his formulations of Christian doctrine and are readily discernable.

6

Assessing Whether Bullinger Authored "the Other Reformed Tradition"

Now that we have considered Bullinger's statement of the doctrine of predestination in the Second Helvetic Confession, we are in a position to return by way of conclusion to the questions that are the focus of this study. When the doctrine of predestination in the Second Helvetic Confession is compared with Bullinger's earlier formulations, do we find confirmation of the thesis that Bullinger's viewpoint underwent a development from an earlier, moderate doctrine of single predestination, to a later, more strict and Calvinistic doctrine of double predestination? This question is related to a broader issue in the study of the doctrinal development of the Reformed tradition in the period of the Reformation and its aftermath: does Bullinger's treatment of the doctrine of predestination represent a substantial departure from or alternative to the doctrine, as it was developed by Calvin and his successors in Geneva? And, if there are important differences between Bullinger and Calvin on the doctrine of predestination, may we attribute these differences to the fact that Bullinger was the author of "the other Reformed tradition," a tradition which emphasizes the centrality of a "conditional" covenant of grace rather than an "unconditional" pre-temporal decree of God?

Though we have already reached some provisional answers to these questions in the preceding chapters, a summary statement of our conclusions is now in order. We will begin with a statement of Bullinger's doctrine of predestination, and then consider the thesis that Bullinger developed his doctrine under the systematic impression of his covenant theology.

A. Bullinger's Doctrine of Predestination: Homiletical Augustinianism

When Bullinger's most important systematic statements on the doctrine of predestination are considered in the historical order of their appearance, there is little or no evidence that his position underwent any kind of substantial modification. Careful study of

Bullinger's formulation of the doctrine at various points throughout the course of his life confirms a remarkable consistency of statement from his earlier to later writings. Even after a period of intense conflict regarding the doctrine of predestination in several of the leading centers of the Reformation, including Zürich itself in the Bibliander and Zanchius conflicts of 1560 and 1561, respectively, Bullinger's handling of the doctrine of predestination evinces no signs of any significant modifications. The argument, therefore, that there is evidence of a shift in Bullinger's position from an earlier moderate view to a later, more strict view, needs to be set aside and should no longer play a significant role in studies of Bullinger's thought.

When the primary themes and emphases of Bullinger's doctrine of predestination are considered, his position might best be characterized as a form of *homiletical Augustinianism.* Bullinger, by means of his frequent citations of Augustine and participation in the debates regarding predestination among the Reformed churches, no doubt self-consciously embraced the fundamental tenets of the Augustinian doctrine of sovereign or gracious predestination. In doing so, he expressed a fundamental concurrence and theological alliance with the doctrine of the other leading Reformers. However, he also exhibited throughout his contributions to these debates a desire to formulate the doctrine within the framework of a keen awareness of its pastoral and homiletical implications. More than some of his contemporaries in the developing Reformed tradition on predestination, he demonstrated a persistent unwillingness to treat the doctrine abstractly, apart from considerations relating to the preaching of the gospel.

Though on some occasions Bullinger treated the doctrine of predestination within the theological locus of divine providence, his formulation of the doctrine was closely linked with the theological loci of soteriology and Christology. Divine pre-destination concerns God's sovereign and gracious purpose to save his people through the person and work of the only Mediator, Jesus Christ. Thus, when Bullinger takes up the doctrine of predestination in the Second Helvetic Confession, he does so within the setting of the doctrine of sin and immediately prior to the doctrine of Christ. The focus of the doctrine in his thought is thereby clearly expressed: fallen sinners have no other hope for salvation than that which is founded upon God the Father's gracious purpose of election in, through, and on account of Christ. The condition of the human will *post lapsum* requires divine monergism in the accomplishment of salvation, not only in the initiative of God's unconditional election in Christ but also in the work of Christ through the gospel, summoning sinners to faith and fellowship with himself. Without exception, Bullinger's formulations of the doctrine of predestination assume this infralapsarian form (God's electing grace alone answers to the sinner's needy condition) and emphasize the sheer graciousness of God the Father's electing purpose in Christ from eternity.

There is, accordingly, no place for any form of synergism in Bullinger's thought. God does not elect his people on the basis of foreseen or foreknown faith. Predestination is not to be confused with God's foreknowledge, but is to be clearly distinguished from it. Without the initiatives of God's grace in Christ and through the summons of the gospel, the sinner is altogether incapable (because sinfully unwilling) to do any saving good or to embrace the gospel promise. When the gospel, which is to be preached to all people, summons sinners to faith and repentance, it is effective only by virtue of God's electing purpose and gracious intention to grant faith and fellowship with Christ to his people. Faith and its corollary, saving fellowship with Christ, are not the product of any work or merit on the part of the sinner, but are themselves the gracious fruits of God's initiative with respect to the elect. According to Bullinger, the theological idiom of divine predestination maintained the sheer graciousness of salvation in Christ. Divine predestination undergirds the administration of the gospel and the communication of the saving grace of Christ by means of the *ordo salutis* or order of salvation.

One particularly vexing issue in the interpretation of Bullinger's doctrine of predestination is the disputed question whether he affirmed only a doctrine of single predestination, identifying predestination exclusively with election, or whether he shared with other Reformed contemporaries, including Calvin, a doctrine of double predestination.[1] Though Bullinger's comprehensive handling of the doctrine of predestination exhibits a remarkable consistency throughout his writings, on the subject of double predestination his formulations are not altogether consistent and reflect a measure of ambiguity.

On several occasions, when setting forth a summary definition of predestination, Bullinger spoke of the double purpose and end of God's counsel. God's predestination or decree is unto salvation and damnation; it includes the particular election of some and the

---

1. Calvin's affirmation of double predestination is clear and unambiguous. Cf. *Institutes,* III.xxi.5: "We call predestination God's eternal decree, by which he compacted with himself what he willed to become of each man. For all are not created in equal condition; rather, eternal life is foreordained for some, eternal damnation for others. Therefore, as any man has been created to one or the other of these ends, we speak of him as predestined to life or to death."

non-election of others. In his *Oratio* of 1536, his letter to Traheronus in the Bolsec matter, his *Decades* of 1549-1551 and, by implication, his concurrence in Bibliander's retirement and signing of the Zürich *Gutachten* of 1561—Bullinger acknowledged that predestination included not only the election of God's people in Christ, but the non-election of others. Therefore, those who maintain that Bullinger affirmed a doctrine of double predestination can appeal with some cogency to these statements. At the least, these statements indicate that Bullinger did not consistently articulate a doctrine of single predestination. However, the evidence for determining whether Bullinger taught double predestination remains somewhat ambiguous. In each case, Bullinger follows his statement of the twofold end of predestination with an argument against any view that would make God the author of the unbelief or impenitence of the non-elect, and so shift the ultimate responsibility for their condemnation to God. Furthermore, in his statements of the doctrine of predestination in his *Summa* and the Second Helvetic Confession, the subject of reprobation was either muted or entirely unmentioned. This ambiguity in the evidence for and against the claim that Bullinger taught a doctrine of double predestination renders a clear resolution of this issue somewhat difficult. At best the evidence warrants no more than a tentative answer to this question.

Perhaps the likeliest explanation for this ambiguity is one which acknowledges that, though Bullinger was willing on occasion to express formally a doctrine of double predestination, he remained particularly concerned to avoid any formulation that would make God responsible for the sinful unbelief of the non-elect or that would hinder the indiscriminate preaching of the gospel to all sinners without exception. Though Bullinger defended a doctrine of double predestination on a few occasions, and was prepared in the disputes of 1560 and 1561 to side with fellow Reformers who clearly affirmed the doctrine, he was concerned to guard against formulations that shifted the responsibility for willful unbelief from the sinner to God, or mitigated the universal promises of the gospel.

Too much should not be made of this anxiety on Bullinger's part, as if this placed him in a position substantially at odds with the doctrine of predestination of his contemporaries. For none of Bullinger's fellow Reformed theologians, including Calvin, taught that God was the author of sin, or that the non-salvation of the reprobate was God's responsibility *in the same manner* in which the salvation of the elect was God's doing. Even Calvin, who stood alone at the time (and subsequently in the Reformed tradition) in his readiness to include the fall into sin within the positive will of God, explicitly rejected the inference that God was the author of human sin or the unbelief and impenitence of the reprobate.[2] Bullinger's resistance to any suggestion that God was the author of sin and evil, was certainly shared at the time by others in the developing Reformed theological tradition. Thus, Bullinger's dislike for any formulation that implied that God was the author of sin or the unbelief of the reprobate does not necessarily mean that he repudiated the doctrine of reprobation altogether. Nor does it mean that his doctrine of predestination was thereby substantially different from, or even at odds with, that of his contemporaries among the Reformed churches.[3]

However, granting that Bullinger may have affirmed in a formal manner the doctrine of reprobation while rejecting the charge that this makes God the author of sin, Bullinger never exhibits any willingness to develop the doctrine of reprobation beyond the confines of his formal definition. He does not formulate the doctrine of reprobation, for example, by means of the scholastic distinction between God's efficient or deficient willing, as was true of Vermigli's doctrine with which he was undoubtedly familiar. Nor does he offer an infralapsarian formulation of the doctrine of reprobation in terms of God's decision to *pass by* (*preterire*) those whom he sovereignly chooses not to save. The subject of reprobation, though explicitly included on several occasions in his formal definition of predestination, simply receives no further elaboration in his thought.

2. See Calvin, *Institutes*, III.xxiii.8-11. Speaking of the condemnation of the reprobate, Calvin insists that its "evident cause" is human sinfulness (III.xxiii.8): "By his own evil intention, then, man corrupted the pure nature he had received from the Lord; and by his fall he drew all his posterity with him into destruction. Accordingly, we should contemplate the evident cause of condemnation in the corrupt nature of humanity—which is closer to us—rather than seek a hidden and utterly incomprehensible cause in God's predestination." Cf. Muller, *Christ and the Decree*, 24-25.

3. Jan Rohls, *Reformed Confessions: Theology from Zurich to Barmen* (Louisville, KY: Westminster John Knox Press, 1997), 153, notes that, in the mainstream of Reformed theology in the sixteenth and seventeenth centuries, the doctrine of reprobation "makes God not the author of sin, but its avenger." This holds true even for supralapsarianism which he describes as the "most logically developed form of an a priori construction of the doctrine of predestination" (152). Baker, *Heinrich Bullinger and the Covenant*, 32-33, *et passim*, frequently cites Bullinger's insistence that God is not the author of sin as tantamount to a repudiation of the doctrine of reprobation. Bullinger's position, however, is more elusive than that. What he clearly rejects is the teaching of a positive relation between God's will and human sinfulness. Whether this means that he rejected any formulation of a doctrine of predestination and reprobation is not as clear.

Indeed, rather than giving any theological account of the subject of reprobation, the primary preoccupation of Bullinger's doctrine of predestination remains God's gracious purpose of election. When the gospel is preached, what always requires emphasis, according to Bullinger, is the goodness of God the Father in his grace and kindness toward sinners in Christ. The keynote to be sounded in the presentation of the gospel is that of God's goodness in inviting sinners without exception to come to Christ in faith, with the promise of salvation attached to this invitation. Thus, what seems peculiarly to characterize Bullinger's handling of the doctrine of predestination is the *homiletical* and pastoral form in which the doctrine is presented. This is apparently what accounts for Bullinger's unwillingness to develop in any theological manner the subject of reprobation. Fearful that the grace of God in Christ might be overshadowed by the specter of an implacable decree of reprobation, Bullinger accents throughout his presentations of the doctrine of predestination the theme of God's goodwill in Christ toward sinners, as this is announced in the preaching of the gospel. Unbelievers may not claim that they are prevented from answering this gospel invitation, except by virtue of their own persistent unbelief and impenitence. Though faith is God's gift to his elect only, unbelief is the culpable response of those who refuse to heed the gospel summons and turn to Christ. It is not so much, then, that Bullinger formally repudiates the doctrine of reprobation, as that he finds it, at least in the form with which he was familiar, something that mitigates the kinds of notes that need to be sounded in the administration of the gospel through preaching.

These homiletical interests undergird the kinds of accents that characterize Bullinger's statement of the doctrine of predestination in the Second Helvetic Confession and throughout his writings. When the promises and warnings of the gospel are faithfully preached, then the most pressing matter concerns the believer's fellowship with Christ on the one hand, or the reprobate's persistent refusal to have any fellowship with Christ on the other. Assurance of election is not to be discovered apart from Christ, the mirror of our election, but only in the context of a believing appropriation of the gospel promise in him. Similarly, the occasion for the condemnation of the wicked is to be discovered particularly in their unbelief, and not ascribed to God's purpose of non-election.

Undoubtedly, many of Bullinger's emphases in his formulation of what I am terming a "homiletical Augustinianism" were not foreign to the writings of the other Reformers of the period. Similar emphases are by no means absent from Calvin's statement of the doctrine.[4] However, in the articulation of his position, Bullinger distinguished his statement of the doctrine of predestination from what he took to be inappropriate emphases in Calvin's works, especially his inclusion of the fall into sin within the scope of God's will or decree. In doing so, he set forth a position which repudiated synergism on the one hand, while stressing the administration and preaching of the gospel to all sinners on the other. Theologically formulated, Bullinger attempted to hold in careful balance both the motifs of *sola gratia* and human responsibility, while disavowing some of the conclusions of those who approached this doctrine in a more rigorous and logical fashion.

This does not mean that Bullinger's position lacked theological integrity. It was always governed by the single theological function mentioned above, namely, to underscore salvation *sola gratia* and *sola fide*. However, Bullinger was disturbed by the way some articulated their doctrine, and interpreted their less cautious and more rigorous approach as casting a shadow over the preaching of the gospel of salvation. While his doctrine shared the same theological function, it did so in such a way as to retain an emphasis upon having a good hope for all, upon proclaiming the gospel to every creature and upon God's desire for the salvation of all. Bullinger endeavored to present the doctrine of election in a manner that included a clear statement that "God is a philanthropos who, on account of his goodness, wants all men to come to salvation and a knowledge of the truth" (*"Deus philantbropos pro bonitate sua vult omnes homines salvos facere, et ad agnitionem veritatis per venire"*).[5]

B. Bullinger on Predestination and Covenant: Another Reformed Tradition?

By arguing that Bullinger's doctrine of predestination was a form of homiletical Augustinianism, we have anticipated in part our evaluation of the claim that Bullinger developed his position under the systematic impression of his doctrine of the covenant. J.

---

4. In Calvin's treatment of the doctrine of election, several of the emphases of Bullinger's doctrine are also present. For example, though Calvin affirms a doctrine of double predestination, he insists that the "cause and occasion" of the condemnation of the reprobate "are found in themselves" (*Institutes*, III.xxiii.8). He also directs believers not to God's secret counsel, but to Christ who is "the mirror wherein we must, and without deception may, contemplate our own election" (*Institutes*, III.xxiv.5). Unlike Bullinger, however, Calvin includes the fall into sin within God's counsel, rejecting the distinction between God's "permissive" and "efficient" will (*Institutes*, III.xxiii.8).

5. *Bullingerus Calvino*, CO 14:210.

Wayne Baker, perhaps the most vigorous exponent of this claim, maintains that the peculiarities of Bullinger's doctrine of predestination are the result of the influence and central place in his system of thought of a doctrine of conditional covenant. Unlike the Augustinian understanding of unconditional predestination, which encouraged a testamentary and monopleuric view of the covenant of grace, Bullinger's understanding of predestination was a kind of "conditional predestinarianism," one which gave greater attention to the conditionality of God's dealing with sinners in history.[6]

In his exposition of this thesis, Baker makes some rather far-reaching assertions regarding Bullinger's doctrine, assertions which, if valid, would indeed place Bullinger outside of the circle of traditional Reformed thinking regarding the doctrine of predestination:

> Bullinger's doctrine of predestination, then, undoubtedly had its ambiguities and, at least from the vantage point of hindsight, its inconsistencies. It must be viewed, however, within the context of the historical development of Reformed thought and theology. On the one hand, the Reformed tradition of Calvinist orthodoxy subordinated the matter of salvation and the covenant to double predestination. The covenant was in actuality God's testament, a unilateral promise of salvation to the elect. It applied only to the elect because Christ's atonement was limited to the elect. For the Calvinists, God's double decree of reprobation was absolute and static. On the other hand, Bullinger stressed the covenant as the vehicle through which God dealt with man; God's election only became binding in history as individuals kept the conditions of the covenant. The covenant, then, was the framework within which *sola fide* and *sola gratia* were understood. The covenant tradition was the other Reformed tradition, which must be distinguished from the incipient Reformed orthodoxy of the second half of the sixteenth century.[7]

According to Baker, not only did Bullinger clearly repudiate a doctrine of double predestination, but he also formulated a doctrine of conditional predestinarianism, including the teaching of a universal atonement, which better conformed to his peculiar interest in the doctrine of the covenant. The substantial differences, accordingly, between Bullinger's doctrine of predestination and that of many of his contemporaries, especially Calvin, were due to the substantially different theological orientation of his system of thought.

6. Baker, *Heinrich Bullinger and the Covenant*, 28, *et passim*.
7. Baker, *Heinrich Bullinger and the Covenant*, 53.

In order to evaluate these claims of Baker, we must first consider briefly Calvin's doctrine of the covenant. Does Baker properly state Calvin's position, when he terms it a "unilateral" or testamentary covenant doctrine? After pausing to consider Calvin's doctrine of the covenant, we will take up more directly the question whether Baker's interpretation of Bullinger's doctrines of predestination and covenant correspond to what we have discovered in the course of our examination of his writings.

Though Baker frequently asserts that Calvin taught a testamentary doctrine of the covenant, which does not include any provision for covenantal "conditions" or obligations, recent studies of Calvin's theology suggest that this is a misreading of Calvin's theology.[8] In Calvin's elaboration of the doctrine of the covenant, particularly in his commentaries,[9] the language of conditionality is frequently used. When God covenants with Abraham and his people, he graciously and unilaterally initiates the covenant relationship, to be sure. But this gracious initiative is accompanied by the stipulation of covenant conditions of faith and obedience, without which the blessings of the covenant cannot be realized. Moreover, where there is covenant breaking or disobedience, God visits his covenant displeasure upon those with whom he covenants.[10] Thus, it is not correct to characterize Calvin's covenant doctrine as "unilateral" and "monopleuric," in contrast to the conditional covenant doctrine of Bullinger. Calvin also affirms the bilateral and dipleuric nature of the covenant.

For example, in his commentary on Genesis 17, which records God's covenant with Abraham, Calvin does not hesitate to speak of

8. See, for example, Bierma, "Federal Theology in the Sixteenth Century," 313-16; Hoekema, "Calvin's Doctrine of the Covenant of Grace," 1-12; idem, "The Covenant of Grace in Calvin's Teaching," 133-61; Lillback, *The Binding of God*, esp. 166-209, 214-30; idem, "The Continuing Conundrum," 42-74; and Elton M. Eeningenburg, "The Place of the Covenant in Calvin's Thinking," *Reformed Review* 10 (1957): 1-22.

9. Cf. Richard A. Muller, *The Unaccommodated Calvin: Studies in the Foundation of a Theological Tradition* (New York: Oxford University Press, 2000), 155, who notes that Baker's interpretation of Calvin's covenant doctrine is largely based upon his discussion of the Old and New Testaments in the *Institutes* (II.x-xi), not upon sources which more fully state Calvin's doctrine: "The *Institutes* does not . . . reflect either the extended discussion of the covenant with Abraham in the commentary on Genesis 17, the highly significant bilateral covenant language of the Deuteronomy sermons, or the careful definition of the Psalms commentary in which Calvin notes how from one perspective the covenant is unconditional and from another, conditional."

10. See, for example, *Institutes*, II.xi.8; III.ii.22; III.xxi.7; John Calvin, *Calvin's Commentaries* (hereafter *Comm.* with biblical ref.; Edinburgh: Calvin Translation Society, 1844-56) Lev. 26:40; and Lillback, *The Binding of God*, 214-30. Lillback cites an extensive number of instances in which Calvin speaks of covenant breaking and its consequences.

the covenant in terms of its stipulations and conditions. Indeed, the covenant relationship, which God establishes with Abraham and his seed, requires mutual fidelity on the part of both parties.

> In making the covenant, God stipulates for obedience, on the part of his servant. . . . For on this condition, he adopts children as his own, that he may, in return, obtain the place and the honour of a Father. And as he himself cannot lie, so he rightly demands mutual fidelity from his own children. . . .

> We have said that the covenant of God with Abram had two parts. The first was a declaration of gratuitous love; to which was annexed the promise of a happy life. But the other was an exhortation to the sincere endeavour to cultivate uprightness, since God had given, in a single word only, a slight taste of his grace; and then immediately had descended to the design of his calling; namely, that Abram should be upright.[11]

Contrary to Baker's claim that Calvin taught a monopleuric doctrine of covenant, the mutuality of the covenant of grace is a theme that runs throughout Calvin's treatment of the doctrine of the covenant.[12] The fellowship between God and his people that the covenant expresses includes mutual responsibilities and obligations.

This does not mean that Calvin regarded faith and obedience as "meriting" God's grace in the covenant relationship. Rather, faith and obedience are themselves the fruit of the gracious working of the Holy Spirit. According to Calvin, "[A]s soon as the ignorant sort hears of the word 'condition,' it appears to them that God makes some payment and that when he shows us any favor, he does it in recompense for our merits."[13] To treat the conditions of the covenant as meritorious profoundly distorts the way in which faith and obedience themselves are produced in us by the Holy Spirit through the gospel.[14] Rather than opposing God's grace to the

---

11. *Comm.* Deut. 17:1-2. Cf. *Institutes*, II.x.8: "For the Lord always covenanted with his servants thus: 'I will be your God, and you shall be my people.' The prophets also commonly explained that life and salvation and the whole of blessedness are embodied in these words. . . . He is our God on this condition: that he dwell among us, as he has testified through Moses."

12. See, for example, *Comm.* Gen. 12:3; Ex. 24:5; Ps. 78:37; 105:11; 122:4; Isa. 24:5; Jer. 22:24; Hos. 2:16, 19-20; Hab. 1:12; Zech. 9:11; Mal. 2:5, 10; Mark 14:24; Rom. 3:3, 29. Cf. Lillback, "The Continuing Conundrum," 63n, who cites these and many other passages that speak of the stipulations and duties of the covenant relationship.

13. *Sermons of Master John Calvin upon the Fifthe Book of Moses called Deuteronomie*, trans. A. Golding (London, 1583), 322 (serm. On Deut. 7:11-15).

14. Cf., for example, *Sermons upon Deuteronomie*, 1175 (serm. On Deut. 32:44-47); *Institutes*, III.xvii.6.

stipulations of covenant faith and obedience, Calvin maintains that these stipulations are realized by the grace of God in the lives of the elect. Moreover, the existence of the covenant relationship is itself altogether according to divine grace, and is based upon the singular initiative of God. Though the conditionality of the covenant of grace and the unconditionality of election may appear to be in tension, Calvin addresses this seeming tension by emphasizing that faith and obedience are simultaneously God's gift and his demand.

The error in Baker's claims regarding Calvin's doctrine of the covenant stems, accordingly, from his failure to see how faith can be regarded in this twofold manner: as both gift and obligation. Because Calvin stresses the sovereign initiative and grace of God in the salvation of the elect, Baker concludes that he fails to do justice to the conditions of the covenant. But this no more follows than that, because Bullinger emphasizes the conditions of the covenant of grace, he teaches, as Baker alleges, a form of "conditional predestinarianism." As we have seen in our treatment of Bullinger's doctrine of election, he, as much as Calvin, insisted that faith is God's gift to his elect, and not a meritorious condition which constitutes the ground for salvation. Furthermore, when Baker argues that Bullinger's *single* predestinarianism allows him to stress the conditionality of the covenant and to ascribe the responsibility for the non-salvation of the reprobate to their unbelief, he seems to imply that Bullinger must have believed that the reprobate are fully capable either of believing or not believing the gospel promise. But this was no more Bullinger's position than it was Calvin's. Bullinger, like Calvin, recognized that the requirements (conditions) of the covenant of grace could only be realized in the elect by the sovereign initiative and working of the Spirit of Christ.[15] As we have seen, this is precisely the point Bullinger makes in arguing that faith is itself a gift of God's grace in Christ to the elect. Consequently, Baker's claims that Calvin's doctrine of double predestination corresponds to a unilateral

---

15. Cf. Bierma, "Federal Theology in the Sixteenth Century," 316: "To suggest, as Baker does, that Calvin resolves this tension [between salvation *sola gratia* and human responsibility] by making faith a gift rather than a condition does justice neither to Calvin's many references to the conditional nature of the covenant nor to Bullinger's own insistence that faith is a gift of God bestowed on those whom he has elected from eternity. . . . Baker implies that Bullinger's single predestination . . . helps to preserve the conditional nature of the covenant because the reprobate, not God, bear final responsibility for their rejection. It is difficult to see, however, how these two views of reprobation affect the conditionality of the covenant. By locating the ultimate cause of reprobation in human *unbelief* Bullinger does not mean to suggest the possibility that reprobate persons after the fall are capable of fulfilling the condition of *belief.*"

doctrine of the covenant, and that Bullinger's doctrine of single predestination corresponds to a bilateral doctrine of the covenant, cannot be sustained.

Perhaps the more basic problem with Baker's interpretation of Bullinger's thought, however, is the claim that Bullinger *systematically organized and structured his theological system under the control of a conditional covenant doctrine.*[16] This approach to Bullinger's theology is remarkably similar in form to the older tradition of nineteenth-century scholarship, which looked for "central dogmas" that were alleged to be the principal themes of the Protestant dogmatic systems of the late sixteenth and seventeenth centuries. Whether in the theologies of the Reformers of the sixteenth century or their epigoni in the period of Protestant scholasticism, these principal doctrines were regarded as the basic points of departure for theological systems derived deductively from them. In the position of Baker and others who argue that Bullinger was a covenant theologian, something like this is true as well of Bullinger's thought: all of its diverse aspects are ordered and influenced by his covenant theology. Thus, if Bullinger taught a doctrine of conditional covenant as the principal and organizing theme of his theology, then his doctrine of predestination must be interpreted accordingly, subordinate as it was to this overriding and principal interest.

There is, however, little evidence that Bullinger systematically organized his theology in this manner, treating the doctrine of the covenant as an "organizing principle of his thought." An examination of Bullinger's primary comprehensive statements of the Christian faith, including all of the sources we have considered in this study, provides little or no evidence for this thesis.[17]

16. Baker, *Heinrich Bullinger and the Covenant,* 48: "Bullinger's doctrine of predestination must be understood within the context of his covenant idea, for his system, such as it was, centered around the covenant. And his covenant notion was based on biblical exegesis and his understanding of how God worked in history, not on logical categories and dogmatic formulations. That is to say, the covenant was not a dogmatic principle in the later Reformed scholastic sense; it was, however, the cornerstone and organizing principle of his thought." Cf. Koch, *Die Theologie der Confession Helvetica Posterior,* 425-30, who likewise claims that covenant was the organizing principle of Bullinger's theology.

17. Dowey, "Heinrich Bullinger as Theologian," 45-46, offers a telling critique of Baker's approach to and claims regarding Bullinger as a covenant theologian: "Although a mosaic of Bullinger materials thus assembled seems to make Baker's point, . . . a broader survey of Bullinger's thought shows not only that this judgment is premature, but possibly that Bullinger in his entire theological lifework never had a single 'principal formative and organizing factor.' . . . My own suggestion is that it may be Baker's consuming interest in both theological and political federalism that leads him to be less concerned

Though Bullinger certainly gave considerable place to the doctrine of the covenant, it is noteworthy that, in several of his most significant and influential works, including his *Decades* and the Second Helvetic Confession, the doctrine of the covenant does not approximate an organizing principle of his thought. This is not to deny the significant place of the doctrine of the covenant in his theology. Nor is it to deny that Bullinger played a most important role in the development of covenant theology in the Reformed tradition. But it is to deny that Bullinger's theology is properly interpreted as principally a form of covenant theology, all of whose themes are governed by the dictates of the covenant of grace.

The problem with this approach to Bullinger's theology, particularly as it relates to his doctrine of predestination, is that it presses Bullinger's thought into a mold that it does not fit. Though Bullinger never provides a systematic treatment of the inter-relation of the doctrines of predestination and covenant, there is enough evidence of the nature of this interrelation in his thought to call the interpretation of Baker and others into question. This can be seen in at least two principal and related areas of his doctrine of predestination: Bullinger's insistence upon the unconditionality of God's purpose of election, an insistence he shared with his fellow adherents to the Augustinian exegetical and theological tradition on predestination; and Bullinger's explicit affirmation that the "conditions" of the covenant of grace are themselves graciously bestowed by God to the elect.

On the subject of unconditional election, it is apparent from all of Bullinger's statements on the doctrine of predestination that God's purpose to elect his people in Christ is not based upon foreseen faith or works. On this most important element in traditional Augustinian teaching, Bullinger was in substantial agreement with the mainstream of the Reformed tradition during the period of his reformatory labor as *Antistes* in Zürich. Any formulation of the doctrine of the covenant, therefore, that would ground the salvation of God's people upon their own response in faith and repentance to the preaching of the gospel would be in substantial conflict with Bullinger's repeated disavowals of synergism or conditional election.[18] Though Bullinger does not

with the problems of Bullinger's thought as a whole, and overly concentrated on a single theme of subsequent great influence. Our problem remains: given these grounds for a covenant program, early and late, why did Bullinger *not* develop such a theology in his principle [sic] comprehensive writings?"

18. Cf. Aurelio A. Garcia Archilla, *The Theology of History and Apologetic Historiography in Heinrich Bullinger: Truth in History* (San Francisco: Mellen Research University Press, 1992), 17, 42-43, 50-51, 67, 314, who argues that Baker's interpretation of Bullinger's emphasis upon the conditionality of the

explicitly address the theological correlation or relation between his doctrines of predestination and covenant, the internal coherence and integrity of his theological thought would be open to considerable doubt, were he to have taught that the conditionality of the covenant requires the inference that salvation is based, in any manner, upon human works or merit. Without stating so explicitly, his consistent repudiation of Pelagian or semi-Pelagian formulations of the doctrine of salvation, together with his frequent references to the Augustinian doctrine of unconditional election, clearly exclude any teaching that would make human faithfulness in covenant with God the putative ground of salvation. Unless there were evidence that Bullinger did not teach in a consistent manner that predestination is a sovereign and unconditioned act of God the Father's grace in Christ, it is incorrect to argue that his covenant doctrine, with its emphasis upon the correlation between salvation and the human response of faith, represented a substantial theological alternative to the Augustinian consensus on predestination.

Furthermore, in his formulations of the doctrine of predestination, Bullinger clearly affirmed that the requirements of the gospel—faith and repentance—are granted by God, in accordance with his purpose of election, to those whom he is pleased to save. Because God sovereignly bestows faith and repentance to the elect by means of the administration of the gospel, Bullinger's emphasis upon the conditionality of the covenant of grace can hardly be construed synergistically. The conditions of the covenant, where these are met by believers in fellowship with Christ, are themselves the fruit of God's gracious purpose of election. Since Bullinger, in his statements of the doctrine of predestination, consistently treats faith, for example, as a gracious bestowal to the elect in Christ, he is able to affirm simultaneously the unconditional character of election and the conditionality of the covenant in its administration through preaching and the sacraments. Admittedly, were he to have treated the covenant conditions of faith and repentance as the ground upon which God determined to save some and not others, he would have had to teach a doctrine of conditional predestination. He would then have taught a kind of "proto-Arminian" doctrine which would have placed him outside of the theological and confessional boundaries of the Reformed

covenant treats Bullinger as though he were semi-Pelagian in his doctrine of grace. Archilla maintains that Baker incorrectly makes covenant the ruling concept of Bullinger's theology, and that he draws inappropriate conclusions from the conditionality of the covenant for an understanding of Bullinger's doctrine of predestination.

114

theological tradition, a tradition of which, as we have seen, he was a significant exponent and defender. But in the writings we have considered in this study, Bullinger consistently treats faith, to which sinners are called through the gospel, as God's gift to his elect, not as a human work which, having been foreseen from eternity, constitutes the basis for God's purpose of election.[19]

Because Bullinger concurred with the Augustinian teachings that predestination is unconditional, and that the faith of the believer is a divine bestowal to those whom God elects to save, too much should not be inferred either from Bullinger's reluctance to develop the doctrine of double predestination or his emphasis upon the universal promises of the gospel. Because faith is God's gift to the elect only, it is incorrect to argue, as Baker does, that Bullinger taught a doctrine of reprobation upon the ground of foreseen unbelief and impenitence, as though the reason some are saved or not saved stems solely from their differing responses to the gospel. Bullinger, despite his reluctance to develop the doctrine of reprobation in any explicit or logically rigorous manner, did not teach that what ultimately distinguishes the elect and reprobate is that one believes and another does not. Though the knowledge of election is correlated with faith in Christ or being outside of Christ, election itself is based only upon God's sovereign and particular purpose to save his people in Christ. What distinguishes the elect and reprobate, therefore, is not simply that one believes and another does not. What distinguishes them is God's purpose of election, which involves his granting faith to some and not others. Thus, even though Bullinger does not articulate the doctrine of reprobation in the manner of some of his contemporaries, his doctrine of predestination is not thereby

---

19. In one of his last treatises, *Von der Bekehrung des Menschen zu Gott* (Zürich: Froschauer, 1569; *HBibl I*, no. 561), fol. 8a, Bullinger clearly affirms that the condition of repentance is something which God graciously grants to the elect: "Es ist zwaren ein frye waal unnd vorsaehung vor Gott von ewigkeit har / der allein sine erwoelten kennt: welche ouch allein uns luterer gnad beruefft und fromm gemacht / selig werdend. Die Apostolische und Evangelische leer aber leert uns nit unsere bekeerung also anheben und raechnen / dass wir sagind / Bin ich von Gott erwollt, so wird ich bekeert / und darff mines thuons nüt darzuo. Bin ich denn nit der erwoellten / sonder der vervorffnen / so hilfft mich nütt / weder glouben noch bekeerung: wil mich desshalb wyter nit unlassen / . . . Dann in aller goettlicher geschrifft findst du kein exempel oder byspil / dass ye einicher Gottes diener / sin raechnung also gemachtet habe." Baker, *Heinrich Bullinger and the Covenant,* 47, cites this treatise in support of his interpretation of Bullinger's teaching. However, he fails to see that it expresses Bullinger's simultaneous affirmation of unconditional predestination and the conditionality of repentance in the administration of the covenant. He also neglects to note that it contains one of Bullinger's strongest statements of double predestination.

substantially different from theirs simply by virtue of his emphasis upon the conditionality of the covenant of grace.

This is also the context within which to address the subject of Bullinger's emphasis upon the universal promises of the gospel. Baker argues that this emphasis stems from Bullinger's covenant doctrine and expresses his teaching of a universal atonement. When the covenant of grace is administered through preaching, a general or universal promise of salvation is extended to all, inviting them to respond in faith to the gospel promise. Because Bullinger insisted that this gospel promise expresses God's good will toward all, often noting that God desires that all should be saved and come to a knowledge of the truth, he believed that the saving work of Christ, particularly his atoning death, was accomplished for all sinners. According to Baker, Bullinger taught that "Christ died for every man and everyone was called to salvation."[20] This teaching of a universal atonement corresponds to Bullinger's emphasis upon the conditionality of the covenant of grace, and illustrates the extent to which his doctrine of predestination was governed by the requirements of his covenant doctrine.

It is certainly true that one of the remarkable features of Bullinger's treatment of the doctrine of predestination is his frequent insistence upon preaching the promises of the gospel to all without distinction. The doctrine of predestination must not be taught or preached, according to Bullinger, in a manner that would undermine the indiscriminate preaching of the gospel's call to faith in Christ with the promise of salvation to all who turn in faith and repentance. Bullinger, as is illustrated in his statement of the doctrine in the Second Helvetic Confession, was displeased with formulations which suggested that the number of the elect was few, or which hindered the free presentation of the gospel of Christ—with its promises, admonitions and warnings—to all sinners. He was anxious to insist that, in the preaching of the gospel, God's goodness and benevolence toward sinners must have

20. Baker, *Heinrich Bullinger and the Covenant*, 46. Baker also draws the following remarkable conclusion from Bullinger's emphasis upon the universal promises of the gospel: "If Bullinger himself had been at Dort, he would have disagreed with both parties. Certainly he would have rejected the high Calvinist assertions of necessity or compulsion and of limited atonement, as expressed in the Canons of Dort. Most likely he would have felt uncomfortable among these uncompromising scholastics. Perhaps he would have been more compatible temperamentally with the Remonstrants. And he might well have agreed in general with their point in the Remonstrance affirming a universal atonement" (47). It should be noted that, contrary to this representation of the Canons, they do not teach, but strongly repudiate, any doctrine of a "compulsion" in the salvation or non-salvation of sinners. See *Canons of Dort*, III/IV, 8-17.

particular prominence. These emphases are undoubtedly central to Bullinger's consideration of the doctrine of predestination, and reflect its character as a form of homiletical Augustinianism.[21]

However, it is an anachronism, and possibly a serious distortion of Bullinger's theology, to maintain that in this or in other respects, Bullinger was *proto-Arminian* in his doctrine of predestination, particularly in teaching a doctrine of universal atonement. Bullinger was a consistent champion of the central theological interest of Augustinianism: the divine purpose of election is an expression of sheer, unmerited and unconditional grace. Thus, on the most basic question confronting the Synod of Dort in 1618-1619, whether the salvation of sinners is founded upon unconditional election or foreseen faith, Bullinger would no doubt have had little difficulty siding with the authors of the Canons. Just as in the disputes of 1560 and 1561 in Zürich, Bullinger would likely have chosen to defend the ancient and catholic teaching of unconditional election, as this had been taught in the tradition of Augustinianism. Whether Bullinger would have agreed or disagreed with the other, related points of contention at the Synod of Dort can only remain a matter of conjecture. It is an unhistorical anachronism, however, to argue that, because of his covenant doctrine, Bullinger would likely have sided with the Remonstrants on the doctrine of universal atonement. Nowhere in his writings does Bullinger address the issue of universalism in the form it was addressed immediately before and after the Synod of Dort in 1618-1619. Thus, it is difficult to know—certainly it can hardly be proven within the limits of historical scholarship—what Bullinger would have

21. These are the kinds of emphases Baker cites to support his claim that Bullinger taught a doctrine of universal atonement, namely, that "Christ died for every man" (46). In particular he appeals to a number of passages in Bullinger's 1567 commentary on Isaiah (*Isaias excellentissimus Dei propheta, cuius testimoniis Christus ipse dominus et eius apostoli* [Zürich: Froschauer, 1567; HBBibl I, no. 558], fol. 8-8b, 10b-11, 36b, 60, 92b, 183, 250b-251, 266b, 275b, 327). Though Baker rightly notes that, in this commentary, Bullinger teaches that "God gave faith to those who desired it and caused the condemnation of no one," he misinterprets Bullinger's emphasis upon God's goodwill toward all as an affirmation of universal atonement. Nowhere in this commentary, including the references cited by Baker, does Bullinger teach that "Christ died for every man." He does affirm that Christ's death was a complete and perfect sacrifice for all of the sins of all men (fol. 266b). But this affirmation, by itself, is not an early precursor of the later Arminian teaching of a universal atonement. It could accommodate the traditional language of Dort that Christ's death is "sufficient for all, but efficient for the elect alone." Bullinger does not address the question of universal atonement in the form it was to take prior to the Synod of Dort in 1618-1619.

contributed to the discussions that emerged subsequent to the period in which he labored as pastor in Zürich.

On the subject of universalism or universal atonement, therefore, the most that can be claimed for Bullinger's doctrine is that he placed special emphasis upon the universal promises of the gospel. To argue from this emphasis that Bullinger taught a doctrine of universal atonement is to claim more than the evidence warrants. There are simply no explicit statements in Bullinger's writing that provide direct support for the claim that he believed Christ's death was provided on behalf of all sinners without exception. Moreover, because Bullinger was quite clear on the matter of unconditional election, it is at least as plausible that, were he to face the question in the form it was posed at Dort, he would have followed the trajectory of his doctrine to the conclusion drawn by the authors of the Canons of Dort: Christ's work as Mediator, by divine design and gracious purpose, provides for the sins of those whom God elects to save. Bullinger's emphasis upon the universal promises of the gospel does not suffice to show that he taught a kind of universal atonement. For not only is this emphasis present in the writings of the other Reformers, including Calvin,[22] but it is also stressed in the Reformed confessions of the Reformation and post-Reformation periods.[23]

C. Summary

Though there is evidence that Bullinger formulated his doctrine of predestination in a manner that was distinct from that of Calvin and as well other Reformed theologians of the period, the distinctiveness of his doctrine does not amount to a substantial divergence of theological position. On the main points of the historic Augustinian doctrine of predestination, Bullinger's doctrine exhibits considerable continuity with the preceding and subsequent tradition of Augustinianism. The theological idiom of predestination expressed in dramatic fashion the monergism of God's sovereign and gracious work in the salvation of his people in Christ. Salvation by grace alone is epitomized in the doctrine of God's gracious and unconditional election from eternity to save his people through the work of the Mediator, Jesus Christ. To posit a fundamental or substantial difference between Bullinger's doctrine of predestination and that of Calvin, accordingly, goes beyond the evidence, and presents too simplistic a picture of the diversity of doctrinal formulation and emphasis among Bullinger's con-

22. Cf., for example, *Institutes,* III.xxiv.15-17.

23. Cf. the summary of the Reformed confessions in Rohls, *Reformed Confessions,* "Particularism and Universalism," 161-66.

temporaries in the emerging Reformed theological tradition of the sixteenth century. At no time in the sixteenth century or subsequently can the Reformed tradition be reduced to the alternatives of Calvin's doctrine of predestination, or one that was substantially at odds with it.

No doubt one of the characteristic features of Bullinger's theology was his development of the doctrine of the covenant of grace. Bullinger, throughout his presentation and formulation of the doctrine of predestination, seems uncomfortable with too speculative or thoroughgoing an analysis of the various aspects of the divine decree. He consistently emphasizes such themes as: God is not the author of sin and unbelief as he is the author of salvation and faith; the condemnation of the reprobate is on account of their own unbelief and impenitence; and the goodwill of God is toward all, manifested in the preaching and promises of the gospel. These characteristic emphases of Bullinger's doctrine of predestination may reflect a theology oriented more especially to the historical administration of the covenant of grace than some of the theological systems of his contemporaries. But that they reflect a fundamentally different theological system, one derived from the dictates of a governing covenant theology, goes beyond anything the evidence will support. For Bullinger, no more than for Calvin or other leading Reformed theologians of the period, the doctrine of predestination, rather than being at odds with the doctrine of the covenant with its conditions, undergirds and sustains the effective working of God's gracious purposes in history. Unconditional election and conditional covenant are not theological antagonists. Rather, election calls for covenant and renders it effective as an instrument of salvation. Unless God graciously grants faith and repentance to his people through the gospel's administration, the requirements of the covenant would only demand what the sinner is incapable of producing.

To argue, therefore, that Bullinger was, by virtue of his covenant doctrine, the author of "the other Reformed tradition," is to overlook substantial continuities between his doctrine and that of the Augustinian tradition. But it is also to interpret Bullinger overly much in terms of subsequent debates in the Reformed tradition regarding the doctrine of predestination. Bullinger's doctrine of predestination is neither proto-Arminian nor a proto-type of the more fully developed doctrine affirmed in the early seventeenth-century confession, the Canons of Dort. Just as there are continuities in the Augustinian tradition of predestinarianism, of which Bullinger's doctrine is an illustration, so there are discontinuities or subsequent developments that go beyond the formulations of an earlier period. The interpretation of Bullinger's

119

doctrine of predestination, in short, needs to be governed by a careful study of his place in the developing tradition of Reformed theology. Furthermore, it needs to be freed from the constraints of other theological interests and motives.

Bibliography

Primary Sources

Bullinger, Heinrich. *Aphorismi de praedestinatione: de causis humanae salutis et damnationis aphorismi ex consensione re sacramentaria ministrorum ecclesiae Tigurinae et Genevensis (1549).* November 27, 1551. In CO 14, col. 209-10.

————. *Der alt gloub. Das der Christen gloub von anfang der waelt gewaert habe.* Zürich, 1539. (*HBBibl I*, no. 99).

————. *Von der Bekehrung des Menschen zu Gott.* Zürich: Froschauer, 1569. (*HBBibl I*, no. 561)

————. *Bullingerus Calvino.* November 27, 1551. In CO 14, col. 207-8.

————. *Bullingerus Calvino.* December 1, 1551. In CO 14, col. 214-15.

————. *Bullingerus Calvino.* February 20, 1552. In CO 14, col. 289-90.

————. *Bullingerus Calvino.* End of March, 1553. In CO 14, col. 510.

————. *Bullingerus Calvino.* May 22, 1553. In CO 14, col. 533.

————. *Bullingerus Calvino.* March 3, 1555. In CO 14, col. 471.

————. *Bullingerus Calvino.* November 2, 1555. In CO 15, col. 852-54.

————. *Confessio et exposito simplex orthodoxae fidei.* In *Bekenntnisschriften und Kirchenordnungen der nach Gottes Wort reformierten Kirche,* ed. Wilhelm Niesel, 219-76. Zürich: Zollikon, 1938. In English translation: *The Second Helvetic Confession.* In *The Book of Confessions.* New York: The United Presbyterian Church in the U.S.A., 1970.

————. *The Decades of Heinrich Bullinger.* 3 vols. Ed. Thomas Harding. Parker Society, Cambridge University, 1849-1852.

————. *Sermonum Decades duae, de potissimis verae religionis capitibus.* Zürich: Froschauer, 1549. (*HBBibl I*, no. 179)

————. *Sermonum decas tertia.* Zürich: Froschauer, 1550. (*HBBibl I*, no. 180).

———. *Sermonum decas quarta.* Zürich: Froschauer, 1550. (*HBBibl I*, no. 181)

———. *Sermonum decas quinta.* Zürich: Froschauer, 1551. (*HBBibl I*, no. 182)

———. *Sermonum Decades quinque.* Zürich: Froschauer, 1552. (*HBBibl I*, no. 184)

———. *Heinrich Bullinger's DIARIUM (Annales vitae) der Jahre 1504-1574. Zum 400. Geburtstag Bullingers am 18. Juli 1904.* In *Quellen zur Schweizerischen Reformationsgeschichte*, vol. 1, ed. Emil Egli. Basel: Basler Buch und Antiquariatshandlung vormals Adolf Geering, 1904.

———. *De gratia Dei iustificante nos propter Christum.* Zürich, 1554. (*HBBibl I*, no. 276)

———. *Isaias excellentissimus Dei propheta ... expositus Homilijs CXC.* Zürich, 1567. (*HBBibl I*, no. 558)

———. *Oratio de moderatione servanda in negotio providentiae, praedestinationis, gratiae et liberi arbitrii.* January 28, 1536. Printed in Hottinger, *Historiae*, 763-827. (*HBBibl I*, no. 721)

———. *Summa Christenlicher Religion.* Zürich: Froschauer, 1556. (*HBBibl I*, no. 283). In Latin translation: *Compendium christianae religionis.* Zürich: Froschauer, 1556. (*HBBibl I*, no. 291)

———. *De testamento seu foedere dei unico & aeterno.* Zürich, 1534. (*HBBibl I*, no. 54)

———. *Trahero Bullingero: de providentia dei eiusdemque praedestinatione, electione ac reprobatione deque libero arbitrio et quod deus non sit autor peccati.* March 3, 1553. In CO 14, col. 480-90.

———. *Heinrich Bullinger Werke*, pt. 2: *Briefwechsel*, vols. 1-7; pt. 3: *Theologische Schriften*, vols. 1-2. Ed. Ulrich Gäbler *et al.* Zürich: Theologischer Verlag, 1973-1995.

Calvin, John. *Calvin's Commentaries.* Edinburgh: Calvin Translation Society, 1844-1856.

———. *The Institutes of the Christian Religion.* Trans. Ford Lewis Battles. Ed. John T. McNeill. 2 vols. Philadelphia: Westminster Press, 1960.

———. *Ioannis Calvini Opera Quae Supersunt Omnia.* 59 vols. Ed. Wilhelm Baum, Eduard Cunitz and Eduard Reuss. Brunswick and Berlin, 1863-1900.

————. *Sermons of Master John Calvin upon the Fifthe Book of Moses called Deuteronomie.* Trans. A. Golding. London, 1583.

Hottinger, Johann H. *Historiae Ecclesiasticae Novi Testamenti.* Vol. 8. Zürich, 1667.

Kingdon, R. M., and Bergier, J. F., eds. *Registres de la compagnie de Genève au temps de Calvin.* Geneva: Droz, 1964.

Vermigli, Peter Martyr. *Loci Communes D. Petri Vermigli.* London, 1576. Editio secunda, 1583.

Secondary Sources

Adam, Gottfried. *Der Streit um die Prädestination im ausgehenden 16. Jahrhundert: Eine Untersuchung zu den Entwürfen von Samuel Huber und Aegidius Hunnius.* Beiträge zur Geschichte und Lehre der Reformierten Kirche, vol. 30. Neukirchen: Neukirchen Verlag des Verziehungsvereins, 1970.

Anderson, Marvin W. "Peter Martyr, Reformed Theologian (1542-1562): His Letters to Heinrich Bullinger and John Calvin," *The Sixteenth Century Journal* 4 (1973): 41-64.

Archilla, Aurelio A. Garcia. *The Theology of History and Apologetic Historiography in Heinrich Bullinger: Truth in History.* San Francisco: Mellen Research University Press, 1992.

Armstrong, Brian. *Calvinism and the Amyraut Heresy: Protestant Scholasticism and Humanism in Seventeenth Century France.* Madison, WI: University of Wisconsin Press, 1969.

————. "Review of Philip C. Holtrop's *The Bolsec Controversy on Predestination,*" *The Sixteenth Century Journal* 25/3 (1994): 747-50.

Baker, J. Wayne. *Heinrich Bullinger and the Covenant: The Other Reformed Tradition.* Athens, Ohio: Ohio University Press, 1980.

————. "Heinrich Bullinger, the Covenant, and the Reformed Tradition in Retrospect," *The Sixteenth Century Journal* 29/2 (Summer 1998): 359-76.

————, and McCoy, Charles S. *Fountainhead of Federalism: Heinrich Bullinger and the Covenantal Tradition, with a translation of De testamento seu foedere Dei unio et aeterno (1534).* Louisville, KY: Westminster/John Knox Press, 1991.

Bierma, Lyle D. "Federal Theology in the Sixteenth Century: Two Traditions," *Westminster Theological Journal* 44/2 (Fall 1983): 304-21.

Bizer, Ernst. *Frühorthodoxie und Rationalismus.* Zürich: EVZ Verlag, 1963.

Blanke, Fritz. "Calvins Urteile über Zwingli," *Zwingliana* 11 (1959): 66-92.

————. "Enstehung und Bedeutung des Zweiten Helvetischen Bekenntnisses." In *400 Jahre Zweites Helvetisches Bekenntnis*, 13-25. Zürich/Stuttgart: Zwingli Verlag, 1966.

————. *Der Junge Bullinger 1504-1531.* Zürich: Zwingli Verlag, 1942.

————, and Leuschner, Immanuel. *Heinrich Bullinger: Vater der reformierten Kirche.* Zürich: Theologischer Verlag, 1990.

The Book of Confessions. New York: The United Presbyterian Church in the U.S.A., 1970.

Büsser, Fritz. "Bullinger, Heinrich." In *Theologische Realenzyklopädie*, ed. Gerhard Krause *et al.*, vol. 7, 375-87. New York: Walter de Gruyter, 1981.

————. *Wurzeln der Reformation in Zürich: Zum 500. Geburtstag des Reformators Huldrych Zwingli.* Leiden: E. J. Brill, 1985.

De Greef, Wulfert. "The Origin and Development of the Doctrine of the Covenant." In *Calvin's Books: Festschrift for Peter De Klerk*, ed. W. H. Neuser, H. J. Selderhuis, and W. van 't Spijker, 323-356. Heerenveen: J. J. Groen en Zoon, 1997.

Donnelly, John Patrick. *Calvinism and Scholasticism in Vermigli's Doctrine of Grace.* Leiden: E. J. Brill, 1976.

————. "Calvinist Thomism," *Viator* 7 (1976): 441-445.

————. "Three Disputed Vermigli Tracts." In *Essays Presented to Myron P. Gilmore.* Vol. 1, *History*, 37-46. Florence: La Nuova Italia Editrice, 1978.

Dowey, Edward A. "Heinrich Bullinger as Theologian: Thematic, Comprehensive, Schematic." In *Calvin Studies V: Presented at a Colloquium on Calvin Studies at Davidson College and Davidson College Presbyterian Church*, ed. John H. Leith, 41-60. January 19-20, 1990.

————. "Der Theologische Aufbau Des Zweiten Helvetischen Bekenntnisses." In *Glauben und Bekennen*, ed. Joachim Staedtke, 205-50. Zürich: Zwingli verlag, 1966.

Eeningenburg, Elton M. "The Place of the Covenant in Calvin's Thinking," *Reformed Review* 10 (1957): 1-22.

Egli, Emil. "Zur Erinnerung an Zwinglis Nachfolger Heinrich Bullinger." *Zwingliana* 1 (1904): 419-50.

Graafland, C. *Van Calvijn tot Comrie. Oorsprong en ontwikkeling van de leer van de verbond in het Gereformeerd Protestantisme.* Parts 1 and 2. Zoetermeer, 1992.

Gooszen, M. A. *Heinrich Bullinger en de strijd over de Praedestinatie.* Rotterdam, 1909.

Gründler, Otto. *Die Gotteslehre Girolami Zanchis und ihre Bedeutung für seine Lehre von der Prädestination.* Neukirchen: Neukirchener Verlag Des Erziehungsvereins GmbH, 1965.

Hall, Basil. "Calvin Against the Calvinists." In *John Calvin: A Collection of Distinguished Essays,* ed. Gervase Duffield, 19-37. Grand Rapids: Eerdmans, 1966.

Heppe, Heinrich. *Die Dogmatik der evangelisch-reformierten Kirche.* Neu durchgesehen und herausgegeben von Ernst Bizer. Neukirchen: Moers, 1935. In translation: *Reformed Dogmatics Set Out and Illustrated from the Sources.* Rev. and ed. Ernst Bizer. Trans. G. T. Thomson. Grand Rapids: Baker, 1978 (1950).

Herkenrath, Erland, ed. *Heinrich Bullinger Werke,* pt. 1: *Bibliographie,* vol. 2: *Beschreibendes Verzeichnis der Literatur über Heinrich Bullinger.* Zürich: Theologischer Verlag, 1977.

Hoekema, Anthony A. "Calvin's Doctrine of the Covenant of Grace," *The Reformed Review* 15 (1962): 1-12.

———. "The Covenant of Grace in Calvin's Teaching," *Calvin Theological Journal* 2 (1967): 133-61.

Hollweg, Walter. *Heinrich Bullingers Hausbuch: Eine Untersuchung über die Anfänge der reformierten Predigtliteature. Beiträge zur Geschichte und Lehre der Reformierten Kirche,* vol. 8. Neukirchen: Verlag der Buchhandlung des Erziehungsvereins, 1956.

Holtrop, Philip C. *The Bolsec Controversy on Predestination, From 1551 to 1555,* vol. 1, books 1 and 2. Lewiston: Edwin Mellen Press, 1993.

Jacobs, Paul. "Die Lehre von Der Erwählung in Ihrem Zusammenhang Mit Der Providenzlehre Und Der Anthropologie im Zweiten Helvetischen Bekenntnis." In *Glauben und Bekennen,* ed. Joachim Staedtke, 258-77. Zürich: Zwingli Verlag, 1966.

————. *Prädestination und Verantwortlichkeit bei Calvin.* Neukirchen, 1937.

James, Frank A., III. "Calvin and Vermigli on Predestination." In *Peter Martyr Vermigli and Predestination: The Augustinian Inheritance of an Italian Reformer,* ed. Frank A. James III, 251-55. Oxford Theological Monographs. Oxford: Clarendon Press, 1998.

————. "Peter Martyr Vermigli: At the Crossroads of Late Medieval Scholasticism, Christian Humanism and Resurgent Augustinianism." In *Protestant Scholasticism: Essays in Reassessment,* ed. Carl R. Trueman and R. Scott Clark, 62-78. London: Paternoster, 1999.

Kendall, R. T. *Calvin and Calvinism to 1649.* New York: Oxford University Press, 1978.

Koch, Ernst. "Die Textüberlieferung Der Confessio Helvetica Posterior Und Ihre Vorgeschichte." In *Glauben und Bekennen,* ed. Joachim Staedtke, 13-40. Zürich: Zwingli Verlag, 1966.

————. *Die Theologie der Confessio Helvetica Posterior. Beiträge zur Geschichte und Lehre der Reformierten Kirche,* vol. 27. Neukirchen: Neukirchen Verlag Des Erziehungsvereins, 1968.

Kolfhaus, W. "Der Verkehr Calvins mit Bullinger." In *Calvinstudien: Festschrift zum 400. Geburtstage Johann Calvins,* ed. Bohatec, 1-33. Leipzig: Verlag von Rudolph Haupt, 1909.

Lillback, Peter. *The Binding of God: Calvin's Role in the Development of Covenant Theology. Texts and Studies in Reformation and Post-Reformation Thought,* gen. ed. Richard A. Muller. Grand Rapids: Baker Book House, 2001.

Lillback, Peter. "The Continuing Conundrum: Calvin and the Conditionality of the Covenant," *Calvin Theological Journal* 29/1 (April 1994): 42-74.

Locher, Gottfried. "Bullinger und Calvin—Probleme des Vergleichs ihrer Theologien." In *Heinrich Bullinger, 1504-1575, Gesammelte Aufsätze zum 400 Todestag,* ed. U. Gäbler and Erland Herkenrath. *Zürcher Beiträge Zur Reformationsgeschichte,* vol. 8, 1-33. Zürich: Theologischer Verlag, 1975.

————. "Grundzüge der Theologie Huldrych Zwinglis im Vergleich mit derjenigen Martin Luthers und Johannes Calvins." *Zwingliana* 8 (1967): 470-597.

Marsden, George M. "Perry Miller's Rehabilitation of the Puritans: A Critique," *Church History* 39 (1970): 99-104.

McClelland, J. C. "The Reformed Doctrine of Predestination According to Peter Martyr," *Scottish Journal of Theology* 8 (1955): 255-71.

McCoy, Charles S. "Johannes Cocceius: Federal Theologian," *Scottish Journal of Theology* 16 (1963): 352-70.

McNeill, John T. *The History and Character of Calvinism.* New York: Oxford University Press, 1965.

Miller, Perry. *Errand into the Wilderness.* New York: Harper Torchbacks, 1964.

———. *The New England Mind: The Seventeenth Century.* New York: MacMillan, 1939.

Moltmann, Jürgen. *Prädestination und Perseveranz: Geschichte und Bedeutung der reformierten Lehre 'de perseverantia sanctorum.'* Neukirchen: Verlag der Buchhandlung des Erziehungsvereins, 1961.

Müller, E. F. K. *Die Bekenntnisschriften der reformierten Kirche.* Leipzig, 1903.

Muller, Richard. "'Calvin and the Calvinists': Assessing Continuities and Discontinuities Between the Reformation and Orthodoxy, Part One," *Calvin Theological Journal* 30/2 (November 1995): 345-75; "'Calvin and the Calvinists': Assessing Continuities and Discontinuities Between the Reformation and Orthodoxy, Part Two," *Calvin Theological Journal* 31/1 (April 1996): 125-60.

———. *Christ and the Decree: Christology and Predestination in Reformed Theology from Calvin to Perkins.* Grand Rapids: Baker, 1988 (1986).

———. "The Myth of 'Decretal Theology,'" *Calvin Theological Journal* 30/1 (April 1995): 159-67.

———. *Post-Reformation Reformed Dogmatics: II. Holy Scripture: the Cognitive Foundation of Theology.* Grand Rapids: Baker, 1993.

———. "Review of Philip C. Holtrop's *The Bolsec Controversy on Predestination*," *Calvin Theological Journal* 29/2 (November 1994): 581-9.

———. *The Unaccommodated Calvin: Studies in the Foundation of a Theological Tradition.* New York: Oxford University Press, 2000.

Niesel, Wilhelm, ed.. *Bekenntnisschriften Und Kirchenordnungen der nach Gottes Wort reformierten Kirche.* Zürich: Zollikon, 1938.

———. *The Theology of Calvin.* Trans. Harold Knight. Reprint, Grand Rapids: Baker, 1980 (1956).

Nijenhuis, W. *Calvinus Oecumenicus.* S'Gravenhage: Martinus Nijhoff, 1959.

Oorthuys, G. *Anastasius' "Wechwyser", Bullingers "Huysboeck" en Calvyns "Institutie" Vergeleken in Hun Leer Van God en Mensch.* Leiden: E. J. Brill, 1919.

Pestalozzi, Carl. *Heinrich Bullinger: Leben und Ausgewählte Schriften. Leben und Schriften der Vater und Begrunder,* vol. 5. Elberfeld: Verlag von R. L. Friderichs, 1858.

Prins, P. "Verbond en Verkiezing bij Bullinger en Calvijn." *Gereformeerde Theologisch Tijdschrift* 56: 97-111.

Ritschl, Otto. *Die reformierte Theologie des 16. und des 17. Jahrhunderts in ihrer Entstehung und Entwicklung. Orthodoxie und Synkretismus in der altprotestantischen Theologie.* Vol. 3. Göttingen: Vandenhoeck & Ruprecht, 1926.

Rohls, Jan. *Reformed Confessions: Theology from Zurich to Barmen.* Trans. John Hoffmeyer. Intro. Jack L. Stotts. *Columbia Series in Reformed Theology.* Louisville, KY: Westminster John Knox Press, 1998 (1987).

Schmidt, C. *Peter Martyr Vermigli. Leben und ausgewählte Schriften.* Elberfeld: Verlag von R. L. Friderichs, 1858.

Schrenk, Gottlob. *Gottesreich und Bund im älteren Protestantismus vornehmlich bei Johannes Coccejus, zugleich ein Beitrag zur Geschichte des Pietismus und der heilsgeschichtlichen Theologie.* 1923. Reprint. Darmstadt: Wissenschaftliche Buchgesellschaft, 1967.

Schweizer, Alexander. *Die Protestantischen Centraldogmen in Ihrer Entwicklung Innerhalb Der Reformierten Kirche. Erste Hälfte, Das 16. Jahrhundert.* Zürich: Orell, Fuessli, 1854.

Staedtke, Joachim, ed. *Heinrich Bullinger Werke,* pt 1: *Bibliographie,* vol. 1: *Beschreibendes Verzeichnis der Gedruckten Werke von Heinrich Bullinger.* Zürich: Theologischer Verlag, 1972.

———. *Die Theologie des jungen Bullinger. Studien zur Dogmengeschichte und systematischen Theologie.* Vol. 16. Zürich: Zwingli Verlag, 1962.

———. "Der Zürcher Prädestinationsstreit von 1560." *Zwingliana* 9 (1953): 536-46.

———, ed. *Glauben und Bekennen. Vierhundert Jahre Confessio Helvetica Posterior. Beiträge Zur Ihrer Geschichte und Theologie.* Zürich: Zwingli Verlag, 1966.

Steinmetz, David C. *Reformers in the Wings.* 1971. Reprint, Grand Rapids: Baker, 1981.

Trinterud, Leonard J. "The Origins of Puritanism," *Church History* 20 (1951): 37-57.

Tylenda, Joseph. "Girolamo Zanchi and John Calvin: A Study in Discipleship as Seen Through Their Correspondence," *Calvin Theological Journal* 10/2 (November 1975): 121-35.

Van't Hooft, Antonius Johannes. *De Theologie van Heinrich Bullinger in Betrekking tot de Nederlandse Reformatie.* Amsterdam: Is. De Hoogh, 1888.

Venema, Cornelis P. "Heinrich Bullinger's Correspondence on Calvin's Doctrine of Predestination, 1551-1553," *The Sixteenth Century Journal* 17/4 (1986): 435-50.

———. "The Twofold Nature of the Gospel in Calvin's Theology: The *duplex gratia dei* and the Interpretation of Calvin's Theology." Ph.D. diss., Princeton Theological Seminary, 1985.

Von Schulthess-Rechberg, G. "Heinrich Bullinger der Nachfolger Zwinglis." *Schriften des Vereins für Reformationsgeschichte* 22/82: 1-104.

Walser, Peter. *Die Prädestination bei Heinrich Bullinger im Zusammenhang mit seiner Gotteslehre. Studien zur Dogmensgeschichte und systematischen Theologie,* ed. Blanke, Rich and Weber, vol. 11. Zürich: Zwingli Verlag, 1957.

Weber, Hans Emil. *Reformatie, Orthodoxie und Rationalismus.* Erster Teil, Zweiter Halbband. *Von Der Reformation Zur Orthodoxie.* 1937-1951. Reprint. Darmstadt: Wissenschaftliche Buchgesellschaft, 1966.

Weir, David A. *The Origins of the Federal Theology in Sixteenth-Century Reformation Thought.* Oxford: Clarendon Press, 1990.

Index

Adam, Gottfried, 21n, 23n
Anderson, Marvin W., 72n
Anthropology, 92, 92n, 93, 94
Antinomianism, 65, 93
Aphorismi de praedestinatione
    (Bullinger—1551), 59, 60, 61
Aquinas, Thomas, 38n, 73n, 74,
    81; predestination as *pars
    providentiae* in his *Summa
    Theologica*, 38n, 92 (*See*
    Scholasticism)
Archbishop Cranmer, 72
Archilla, Aurelio A. Garcia, 113n
Aristotle, 35n, 73n
Arminian (*See* Remonstrants)
Armstrong, Brian G., 25n, 58n
Assurance of salvation, 31n, 45,
    83, 96, 97, 98, 99, 106 (*See*
    Speculum)
Augustine, St., 30n, 36n, 40,
    40n, 52, 55n, 63, 65, 66, 84,
    85, 86, 87, 86n, 97, 97n,
    102, 114, 115, 117; author of
    a theological and exegetical
    tradition, 11, 12, 30n, 54,
    55, 55n, 57, 69, 69n, 73n,
    87, 97n, 113, 118, 119;
    testamentary view of
    covenant, 30, 31, 108; taught
    double predestination, 30, 31
    (*See* Baker, Calvin, Covenant,
    Homiletical Augustinianism)

Baker, J. Wayne, 12, 18n, 27,
    27n, 30, 30n, 31n, 32, 39n,
    66n, 77n, 79n, 82n, 85n,
    99n, 100n, 105n, 107, 108,
    108n, 109n, 111n, 112n,
    113n, 115, 115n, 116, 116n,
    117n; advocate of "two
    covenant traditions" thesis,
    29, 30, 31, 32, 36, 36n, 37,

107, 108, 109, 110, 111,
    112, 113
Barth, Karl, neo-orthodox
    theology, 25; influence upon
    interpretation of Reformed
    tradition, 25; Christo-
    monism of, 26
Basle, 58
Battles, Ford Lewis, 39n
Belgic Confession, 91n
Bergier, J. F., 58n
Berne, predestination conflict of
    1588, 23n, 58, 58n
Beza, Theodore, 23n, 25, 94
Bibliander, 38n, 77n, 78n, 102;
    dispute with Vermigli, 71, 75,
    76, 77, 78, 79; retirement of,
    21, 22n, 33, 75, 76, 78, 79n,
    80, 86, 104; doctrine of
    predestination, 75, 76, 76n,
    77, 78, 79, 102
Bierma, Lyle D., 28n, 29n, 30n,
    109n, 111n
Bizer, Ernst, 24n, 25n
Blanke, Fritz, 18n, 20n, 21n,
    58n
Bohatec, 20n
Bolsec, Hieronymus, 33, 57,
    58n, 61, 62, 62n, 77, 103;
    Bullinger's correspondence
    with Calvin regarding, 58, 59,
    60, 61, 62, 63, 94
Breitinger, Johann Jacob, 80n
Brenz, 58, 84
Bucer, Martin, 72, 73n, 84, 85
Bullinger, Heinrich, Zwingli's
    successor in Zürich, 11, 17,
    36n, 38, 57, 71; *Antistes* in
    Zürich, 12, 35, 36n, 41, 80n,
    89, 113; role in the Reformed
    tradition, 18; doctrine of
    predestination, 20, 21, 22,

38, 39, 44, 86; theologian of
the covenant, 20, 21, 22, 23,
24, 25, 26, 27; doctrine of
unconditional election, 31n;
doctrine of double
predestination, 39, 44, 104;
doctrine of conditional
covenant, 31, 107; relation of
predestination and covenant,
107, 108, 109, 110, 111,
112, 113, 114, 115, 116,
117, 118 (*See* Covenant,
Diarium, Predestination,
Providence, Traheronus)
Büsser, Fritz, 18n, 36n

Call of the Gospel (*See* Universal
Promises of the gospel)
Calvin, John, 11, 12, 17, 17n,
19, 22, 22n, 23, 23n, 24, 25,
26, 26n, 27, 27n, 28, 28n,
29, 30n, 33, 39n, 43n, 49,
54, 55n, 58, 61, 62, 62n, 63,
64, 65, 66, 67, 68, 69, 71,
72, 75, 77, 77n, 78n, 79n,
81n, 85, 87, 89, 94, 97, 99,
101, 103, 103n, 104, 105n,
107, 107n, 108, 109, 109n,
110, 110n, 111, 111n, 118,
119; doctrine of predestination and election, 12, 20,
24, 26, 30, 49, 57, 79, 86,
87, 107n; Calvin and the
Calvinists, 18; theologian of
predestination, 27; predestination a central dogma, 24,
26, 32; Christocentric
theology of, 25; taught
doctrine of double predestination, 30, 60, 68 (*See*
Covenant, Institutes, Double
Predestination, Predestination, Rhineland Reformers)
Canons of Dort, 48, 49, 116n,
118, 119 (*See* Synod of Dort)
Capito, 76, 84
Catholicity of the Reformation,
42, 42n, 43n, 61n, 89, 90n,
91, 117

Central dogma, 24, 25, 27n, 112
(*See* Calvin, Predestination)
Ceporinus, 76
Christ, 21n, 26n, 27n, 29, 31,
31n, 37, 37n, 39, 39n, 40,
41, 43, 44, 45, 45n, 46, 46n,
47, 48, 48n, 49, 50, 51n, 52,
52n, 54, 54n, 59n, 60, 61,
61n, 62, 62n, 67n, 68, 69,
69n, 73n, 74, 74n, 75n, 77n,
80, 81, 81n, 87, 91, 91n, 92,
92n, 93n, 95, 95n, 96, 96n,
97, 97n, 98, 98n, 99, 100,
102, 103, 104, 105n, 106,
107n, 114, 115, 116, 117,
117n, 118 (*See* Mediator,
Speculum)
Christology, 26n, 36, 36n, 38n,
47, 51n, 53, 92, 92n, 97, 102
Clark, R. Scott, 73n
Colladon, 94
College of St. Thomas, 80
Confessio Helvetica Posterior (*See*
Second Helvetic Confession)
Consensus Tigurinus (1549), 59,
60
Consilium (Counsel, Decree) of
God, 60n, 61, 67, 73
Covenant of grace, 19, 20, 22,
27, 28, 29, 30, 30n, 31, 32,
35n, 37n, 39n, 43n, 51, 51n,
52, 53, 55, 55n, 59n, 69n,
99, 99n, 100, 100n, 101,
107, 108, 109, 109n, 110,
110n, 111, 111n, 112, 112n,
113, 113n, 114, 115n, 116,
117, 118, 119; Calvin's view
of, 108, 109, 110, 111; small
place in Second Helvetic
Confession, 99; Puritan view
of, 28; view of Rhineland
Reformers, 29; unconditional
testamentary view of, 32,
109, 110, 111; central theme
of Bullinger, 51, 112, 113;
instrumental to salvation of
the elect, 55, 55n, 100, 119;
conditions of, 55, 109, 113;
relation to predestination in

Bullinger, 107, 108, 109,
110, 111, 112, 113, 114,
115, 116, 117, 118 (*See*
Baker, Bullinger, Miller,
Trinterud)
Covenant theologian (*See*
Bullinger)

Decades (Bullinger—1549-51),
36, 36n, 41, 41n, 42, 42n,
43, 43n, 44, 44n, 45, 45n,
46, 46n, 47, 47n, 48, 48n,
49, 49n, 50, 50n, 52, 53, 55,
57, 59, 66, 66n, 68, 84, 92,
95, 103, 113; structure of,
42; *Hausbuch*, translation of,
42n
De Providentia (Zwingli), 58, 61,
62n
*De providentia Dei eiusdemque
praedestinatione electione ac
reprobatione* (Bullinger), 64;
confusion regarding, 64n
*De testamento seu foedere Dei
unico et aeterno* (Bullinger—
1534), 27n, 43n, 55
Diarium (of Bullinger), 18n, 64n,
78, 78n, 79n, 89n, 90n
Donnelly, John Patrick, 27n,
64n, 73n, 75n, 76n
Double predestination, 23, 30,
37, 39, 44, 49, 53, 54, 58,
60, 66, 66n, 68, 76, 78, 101,
103, 103n, 104, 107n, 108,
111, 115, 115n (*See* Calvin,
Predestination, Reprobation)
Dowey, Edward A., Jr., 11, 13,
17n, 35n, 42, 42n, 43n, 50n,
90n, 91n, 92n, 99n, 112n

Eeningenburg, Elton M., 109n
Egli, Emil, 18n, 21n
Election, 19, 20, 23, 24, 26, 30n,
31, 31n, 32, 37, 37n, 39,
39n, 41, 43, 45, 46, 47, 48,
50, 52, 53, 54, 54n, 55, 59,
60, 59n, 64, 64n, 66, 66n,
67, 68, 69, 72, 73, 74, 75,
76, 77, 77n, 80, 81, 82, 85,

87, 89, 92, 94n, 95, 96, 97,
98, 99, 100n, 102, 103, 104,
106, 107, 107n, 108, 111,
113 (*See* Predestination)
England, 64, 72
Erasmus, 37, 38n, 76

Faith, 31, 41, 43, 43n, 46, 49,
49n, 50, 54, 55, 59, 60, 69n,
77, 79, 80, 81n, 85, 89, 90,
90n, 97, 102, 103, 106, 109,
110, 111, 111n, 112, 117n;
foreseen, 31n, 40, 54, 66, 67,
103, 113, 115, 117; God's gift
to the elect, 31n, 47, 54, 54n,
62, 67, 68, 82, 84, 95, 96,
100, 106, 111, 114, 115,
119; sign of election, 45, 54,
68 (*See* Assurance of salvation, Sola fide, Speculum)
Fall of Adam, 39n, 47, 52n, 63,
63n, 67, 68, 81n, 93, 94,
104, 105n, 107, 107n, 111n
Farel, 62n
First Helvetic Confession (1536),
18n, 89
Florence, Italy, 72
Freedom of the will, 31, 38n, 39,
41, 66, 73, 93; threefold
status of, 65, 93; *ante et post
lapsum*, 40, 65, 93, 102; (*See*
Monergism, Synergism, Will
of God)

Gäbler, Ulrich, 21n, 35n
Geneva, 11, 12, 29, 54, 57, 58,
59, 60, 61, 62, 64n, 94, 101;
controversy regarding
Bolsec's teaching, 77
Genevan Senate, 58, 59, 60
God, not the author of sin, 38,
39, 40, 54, 55, 58, 62, 63,
65, 68, 69, 95, 104, 105,
107, 119; a *philanthropos*,
59, 61n, 68, 96, 107; wants
all to be saved, 59, 68; an
amator hominum, 45n, 67,
67n; *locus Deo*, 81 (*See* Universal promises, Will of God)

Golding, A., 110n
Gooszen, M. A., 21n
Gratia inamissibilis, 83, 84 (*See*
  Preservatio sanctorum)
Gregory of Rimini, 73n
Gründler, Otto, 81n
Gutachten (*See* Zürich
  Gutachten)

H. Henry Meeter Center for
  Calvin Studies, 13
Hall, Basil, 25n
Haller, Wolfgang, 82
Harding, Thomas, 42n
Heppe, Heinrich, 24, 24n
Herkenrath, Erland, 21n
Hoekema, Anthony A., 30n,
  109n
Hollweg, Walter, 21n, 22n, 42n,
  47n, 82n, 85n, 86, 86n
Holtrop, Philip C., 58n
Homiletical Augustinianism,
  101, 102, 103, 104, 105,
  106, 107, 117
Hottinger, Johann H., 37n
Huber, 23n

Infant baptism, 99
Infralapsarian, 51n, 52n, 75, 81,
  81n, 82n, 92, 95, 103, 105
  (*See* Predestination)
Institutes of John Calvin, 35,
  39n, 59, 61, 73, 97n, 103n,
  105n, 107n, 109n, 110n,
  118n
Isidore of Seville, 36n

Jacobs, Paul, 25n, 92n
James, Frank A., III, 73n, 74n
Joseph Regenstein Library, 13
Justification, 25, 40n, 43, 47,
  50, 51, 54n, 59, 91 (*See*
  Faith, Sola fide)

Kendall, R. T., 25n
Kingdon, R. M., 58n
Koch, Ernst, 21n, 22n, 35n,
  89n, 90n, 94, 94n, 99n, 112n
Kolfhaus, W., 20n, 21n, 64n

Krause, Gerhard, 36n
Lavater, 82
Leith, John H., 17n
Leuschner, Immanuel, 18n
Lillback, Peter, 27n, 28n, 30n,
  109n, 110n
Limited atonement, 48, 108,
  116n (*See* Synod of Dort,
  Universal Atonement)
Locher, Gottfried, 21n, 43n, 46n
Loci Communes, of Melancthon,
  35; of Vermigli, 64n, 73
Loci, 24, 43, 55, 81, 102; method
  of, 35n
Lord's Supper, 80, 81
Luther, Martin, 17, 38, 38n,
  43n, 49, 84, 87
Lutheran Reformation, 17, 24,
  80, 81, 85; basic
  commitment to justification,
  25

Marbach, Johannes, 79, 80, 81,
  82, 83, 84, 85, 86; vigorous
  defender of the Lutheran
  faith, 80 (*See* Zanchius,
  Zanchius-Marbach dispute of
  1561)
Marsden, George M., 28n
Masson, Robert, 73
McClelland, J. C., 73n
McCoy, Charles S., 25n, 27n, 29
McNeill, John T., 39n, 86n
Mediator, 100, 118 (*See* Christ)
Medieval tradition, exegetical
  and theological, 25;
  scholastic, 73n, 81
Melanchthon, Philip, 35, 37,
  38n, 58, 64, 64n, 72;
  nonpredestinarian theology
  of, 24; synergism of, 65
Merit (or Works), 37, 39, 39n,
  40, 50, 51, 54n, 59, 60, 59n,
  60n, 61n, 67, 74, 87, 91,
  95n, 103, 110, 111, 113,
  114, 117
Miller, Perry, 28, 28n (*See*
  Covenant)
Moltmann, Jürgen, 27n

Monergism, 54, 87, 93, 93n, 95, 102, 118
Muller, Richard, 13, 25, 26n, 27n, 51n, 52n, 58n, 73n, 75n, 81n, 91n, 93n, 105n, 109n
Müller, E. F. K., 90n
Myconius of Basel, 76n, 77, 77n

Niesel, Wilhelm, 25n, 91n
Nijenhuis, W., 58n
Nonpredestinarian theology, 24

Oecolampadius, 76
Oratio de moderatione servanda in negotio providentiae, praedestinationis, gratiae et liberi arbitrii (Bullinger—1536), 31n, 36, 37, 37n, 38, 38n, 39, 39n, 40, 40n, 41, 43, 44, 50n, 52, 53, 66n, 68, 92, 95, 103
Ordo salutis, 103
Orthodoxy (*See* Reformed orthodoxy)

Patristic tradition, 25
Paul, St., the apostle, 37n, 40, 47, 66n, 97
Pelagian, 77n, 113, 114, 114n
Pellikan, Konrad, professor of Old Testament at the Zürich academy, 72, 76
Pestalozzi, Carl, 18n, 64n, 90n
Pighius, 64
Predestination, 47; focal point for evaluation of Bullinger's theology, 19; history of debate regarding Bullinger's view, 18, 19, 20, 21, 22, 23, 24, 25, 26, 27, 28, 29, 30, 31, 32; older literature comparing Bullinger and Calvin, 20, 21, 22, 23; Bullinger's view more practical than Calvin's, 21; Bullinger's view a homiletical Augustinianism, 101, 102, 103, 104, 105, 106, 107;

predestination in Christ, 44, 45, 52; debate regarding Calvin's view, 23, 24, 25, 26; elements of Calvin's view, 23; three major approaches to Calvin's view, 24, 25, 26; includes use of means, 49; Arminius' doctrine of, 47; Vermigli's view of, 72, 73, 74, 75; Bibliander's doctrine of, 76 (*See* Augustine, Bullinger, Calvin, Double Predestination, Election, Zürich Conflict of 1560)
Preservatio sanctorum (preservation of the saints), 47, 48, 48n, 49, 49n, 81, 82, 84, 85, 86 (*See* Synod of Dort)
Princeton Theological Seminary, 11
Prophezei of Zürich pastors, 42
Providence, 41, 47, 50, 51, 64, 65n, 91, 92n, 93, 93n; Epicurean denial of, 92; Pelagian view of, 38; Manichean view of, 38; Bullinger's definition of, 38, 38n, 39, 43, 44, 92, 93; predestination part of, 43, 102; use of means in, 38, 43, 44, 44n, 45, 46, 49, 54, 55, 65, 93, 99, 114 (*See* Aquinas)
Providentia (Zwingli), 58, 61, 62n
Providentia specialis, 43, 53, 92 (*See* Aquinas)
Puritan view of covenant, 28, 29 (*See* Miller, Trinterud)

Rationalistic theology, 25, 73 (*See* Reformed orthodoxy)
Reformed orthodoxy, 20n, 21n, 22, 23, 24, 25, 25n, 26, 26n, 43, 61, 61n, 79, 89n, 108; contrast with Calvin's Christocentric theology, 25; recast Calvin's theology in a scholastic form, 26
Regeneration, 55n, 93, 94n

Remonstrants (Arminian), 22n, 47, 48, 49n, 80, 80n, 114, 116n, 117, 119

Repentance, 41, 43, 46, 54, 55, 55n, 69n, 91, 103, 113, 114, 115n, 116, 119

Reprobation, 24, 31, 39, 39n, 40n, 53, 54, 55, 55n, 59n, 60n, 64, 66n, 69, 72, 73, 74, 75, 75n, 81, 82, 83n, 84, 85, 86, 87, 95, 96, 98, 104, 105, 105n, 106, 108, 111n, 115, 116; decree of, 52, 73, 74, 82, 82n, 85, 87, 96, 98, 104, 105, 106, 111n, 115, 119 (*See* Double predestination)

Reprobos, 59n, 62, 62n, 66n, 67, 67n, 96, 96n, 98

Rhineland Reformers, 12, 17, 28, 30; conditional covenant doctrine, 28, 29; contrast with Calvin's covenant doctrine, 29

Ritschl, Otto, 20n, 21n, 64n, 72, 72n, 73n, 85n

Rohls, Jan, 105n, 118n

Schmidt, C., 72n

Scholasticism, 25n, 27n, 73n, 76n, 92, 105; Reformed, 18, 73n, 81, 112 (*See* Reformed orthodoxy)

Schrenk, Gottlob, 22n

Schweizer, Alexander, 21, 21n, 22, 22n, 24, 24n, 37n, 64n, 71, 72, 72n, 73n, 76n, 80, 81n, 84, 85n, 86, 86n; Schleiermacherian system of, 24

Scotus, Duns, 73n

Second Helvetic Confession (Bullinger—1566), 12, 18n, 22n, 33, 35n, 36n, 90n, 91, 91n, 94, 98, 99n, 101, 102, 113, 116; occasion and purpose, 89, 90, 91; place of predestination, 91, 92, 93, 94, 95; structure of, 91; doctrine of predestination,

89, 95, 96, 97, 101, 104, 106; Geneva's endorsement of, 94

Semi-Pelagian (*See* Pelagian)

Simler, 82

Sola fide (faith alone), 26, 30, 47, 51, 54n, 74, 91, 107, 108 (*See* Faith, Justification)

Sola gratia (grace alone), 19, 30, 37, 41, 46, 47, 69, 107, 108, 111n; theme of, 11, 12, 19;

Sola scriptura, 91

Solo Christo (Christ alone), 47, 51, 69; theme of, 26

Soteriology, 42, 47, 51n, 53, 92, 97n, 102

Speculum, 97, 97n, 98, 106, 107n (*See* Assurance of salvation)

Staedtke, Joachim, 21, 21n, 22n, 35n, 36, 37, 36n, 37n, 75, 76, 76n, 78, 78n, 79, 86, 89n, 90n, 92n

Steinmetz, David C., 11n, 18n, 35n, 72n

Strassburg, 72, 78n, 80, 81, 85, 86

Sturm, J., 86

Summa Christlicher Religion (Bullinger—1556), 36, 49, 49n, 50, 50n, 51, 51n, 52, 52n, 53, 54n, 55, 68, 92, 104; structure of, 50, 51; covenant of grace a central theme, 51, 55 (*See* Covenant)

Summa theologica, of Aquinas, 38n

Supralapsarian, 81n, 82n, 105n

Switzerland, 17, 71, 78, 82; Reformed churches of, 85, 89

Synergism, rejection of, 31, 41, 46, 64, 87, 103, 107, 113 (*See* Freedom of the will)

Synod of Dort, 1618-1619, 23n, 47, 48, 49, 80, 80n, 116n, 117, 117n, 118, 119 (*See* Canons of Dort)

Thomson, G. T., 24n

Traheronus, Bartholomäus, 33, 57; correspondence with Bullinger, 46n, 63, 64, 64n, 65, 66, 67, 68, 71, 84, 92, 94, 95, 103

Trinterud, Leonard J., 28, 28n, 29, 29n

Trueman, Carl R., 73n

Tylenda, Joseph, 78n, 81n

Unconditional election, 31n, 55, 69, 87, 102, 108, 113, 114, 117, 118, 119 (*See* Synod of Dort)

Universal atonement, 108, 116, 116n, 117, 117n, 118 (*See* Limited atonement)

Universal promises of the gospel, 83, 84; emphasized by Bullinger, 31, 47, 48, 63, 67, 68, 69, 82, 96, 104, 107, 115, 116, 116n, 118 (*See* Will of God)

Van't Hooft, Antonius Johannes, 21n, 22n

Venema, Cornelis P., 26n

Vermigli, Peter Martyr, 22, 22n, 27n, 64n, 72n, 73n, 74n, 75, 75n, 76, 76n, 77, 77n, 78, 78n, 79, 79n, 80, 80n, 82, 83n, 84, 85, 86, 87, 105; doctrine of predestination, 72, 73, 73n, 74, 75, 78, 79n, 87; professor of Old Testament and expert in linguistics, 76; Regius Professor of Divinity at Oxford, 72; dispute with Bibliander, 71 (*See* Bibliander, Zürich *Gutachten*)

Walser, Peter, 19n, 21n, 22n, 37n, 38n, 43, 43n, 58n, 64n, 82n

Weber, Hans Emil, 21n, 22n, 24, 24n

Westminster Confession of Faith, 91n

Wick, 82

Will of God, no fatal necessity, 60, 61, 73; distinction between will of permission and of operation, 65, 94n; distinction between "efficient" and "permissive" will, 74, 75, 87, 105, 107n, 117n; no compulsion or absolute necessity of, 41, 54, 83, 84, 85, 93, 95, 116n; relation to reprobation, 54, 55, 66, 73, 74, 93n; desires salvation of all, 53, 68, 76, 116, 119 (*See* Freedom of will, Predestination, Reprobation, Universal promises of the gospel)

Wittenberg, 81

Wolf, Gualter, 82

Works (*See* Merit)

Zanchius, Girolamo, 78n, 79, 80, 81, 81n, 82, 83, 84, 85, 86, 86n, 87 (*See* Zanchius-Marbach dispute of 1561, Marbach)

Zanchius-Marbach dispute of 1561, 23n, 71, 79, 80, 81, 82, 83, 84, 85, 86, 102, 117

Zürich, 17, 36, 57, 58, 59, 60, 61, 63, 71, 72, 76n, 77, 78n, 79, 80, 82, 102, 117;

Zürich Academy, 22, 33, 72, 75, 76, 77, 77n, 78, 79, 86

Zürich, conflict of 1560, 21, 22n, 75, 76, 77, 78, 79, 102, 117 (*See* Bibliander, Predestination)

Zürich *Gutachten* (opinions) of 1561, 22, 22n, 33, 71, 79, 80, 81, 82, 83, 84, 85, 86, 80n, 82n, 83n, 104

Zwingli, Ulrich, 17, 17n, 18n, 19n, 21n, 35, 36n, 38, 38n, 43, 43n, 46n, 49, 57, 58, 58n, 59, 61, 62, 62n, 71, 72, 76, 82, 87 (*See* De Providentia)